How Can Computational Linguistics Improve Information Retrieval?

(CLIIR 2006)

Workshop held in conjunction with COLING/ACL 2006

Sydney, Australia
23 July 2006

ISBN: 978-1-61738-506-3

Printed from e-media with permission by:

Curran Associates, Inc.
57 Morehouse Lane
Red Hook, NY 12571

Some format issues inherent in the e-media version may also appear in this print version.

Printed by Curran Associates, Inc. (2010)

Association for Computational Linguistics
209 N. Eighth Street
Stroudsburg, Pennsylvania 18360

Phone: 1-570-476-8006
Fax: 1-570-476-0860

acl@aclweb.org

Additional copies of this publication are available from:

Curran Associates, Inc.
57 Morehouse Lane
Red Hook, NY 12571 USA
Phone: 845-758-0400
Fax: 845-758-2634
Email: curran@proceedings.com
Web: www.proceedings.com

Table of Contents

Preface

There has been a long standing interest in using various forms of deep natural language processing to improve information or document retrieval. We have a Cambridge Language Research (CLRU) memo from 1964 by Yorick Wilks which describes an application to text searching of a clear precursor of his later well-known machine translation system. We are also aware of even earlier work in the CLRU on information retrieval by Karen Sparck Jones and Margaret Masterman.

This interest has continued right up to the present day, but successes have been few and far between. In general search engines are based on statistical modeling of documents which lacks at least transparent and visible knowledge of language in any conventional sense. Although many continue to believe search engines which do not, for example, recognise that words have multiple senses, cannot do a good job of the task of matching queries and documents, the fact is that most of the time most users of Google find enough relevant documents in the first page or two of hits without such linguistic sophistication.

Computational Linguistics has progressed enormously in the past few years. CL has made significant contributions to the specialised areas of information retrieval, most notably question answering. However, the dominant use model for information retrieval remains the classic search engine task, in which a short key word query is used to generate a ranked list from a pre-indexed heterogeneous collection of documents, and very little work from computational linguistics has been used in the development of these engines.

This workshop will provide a forum to discuss why this is the case, and how to achieve a better take up of what computational linguistic technology within the search engine community.

We would like to thank our two invited speakers, Jamie Callan and Cécile Paris, in particular Jamie who traveled from the US to Australia especially to take part in the workshop, all the authors (whether their papers were accepted or not) and our program committee. The workshop could not have happened without your efforts!

We would like to acknowledge the kind sponsorship of the Cambridge University Press.

John Tait and Michael Oakes
June 2006

Organizers

Chair:

John Tait, University of Sunderland, UK

Co-Chair:

Michael Oakes, University of Sunderland, UK

Program Committee:

Branimir Boguraev, IBM, USA
Stephen Clark, University of Oxford, UK
Bruce Croft, UMass Amherst, USA
Hang Cui, National University of Singapore
Gael Dias, University of Beira Interior, Portugal
Rob Gaizauskas, University of Sheffield, UK
Alexander Gelbukh, National Polytechnic Institute, Mexico
Rosie Jones, Yahoo, USA
Noriko Kando, NII, Japan
Mirella Lapata, University of Edinburgh, UK
Liz Liddy, Syracuse University, USA
Lucia Rino, UFSCAR, Brazil
Mark Sanderson, University of Sheffield, UK
Karen Sparck Jones, University of Cambridge, UK
Chris Stokoe, University of Sunderland, UK
Tomek Strzalkowski, University at Albany, USA
Simone Teufel, University of Cambridge, UK
Olga Vechtomova, University of Waterloo, Canada

Invited Speakers:

Jamie Callan, Carnegie Mellon University, USA
Cécile Paris, CSIRO, Sydney, Australia

Workshop Program

Sunday, 23 July 2006

7:45–8:45 Registration

8:45–9:00 Opening Remarks

9:00–10:00 Invited Talk by Jamie Callan

Session 1: Accepted Paper

10:00–10:30 *Indonesian-Japanese CLIR Using Only Limited Resource*
Ayu Purwarianti, Masatoshi Tsuchiya and Seiichi Nakagawa

10:30–11:00 Coffee

11:00–12:00 Invited Talk by Cécile Paris

Session 2: Accepted Paper

12:00–12:30 *Hybrid Systems for Information Extraction and Question Answering*
Rodolfo Delmonte

12:30–14:00 Lunch

Session 3: Accepted Papers

14:00–14:30 *Extracting Key Phrases to Disambiguate Personal Name Queries in Web Search*
Danushka Bollegala, Yutaka Matsuo and Mitsuru Ishizuka

14:30–15:00 *How to Find Better Index Terms Through Citations*
Anna Ritchie, Simone Teufel and Stephen Robertson

15:00–15:30 *Exploring Semantic Constraints for Document Retrieval*
Hua Cheng, Yan Qu, Jesse Montgomery and David A. Evans

15:30–16:00 Coffee

16:00–17:00 Discussion led by John Tait

Indonesian-Japanese CLIR Using Only Limited Resource

Ayu Purwarianti **Masatoshi Tsuchiya** **Seiichi Nakagawa**
Department of Information and Computer Science, Toyohashi University of Technology
ayu@slp.ics.tut.ac.jp tsuchiya@imc.tut.ac.jp nakagawa@slp.ics.tut.ac.jp

Abstract

Our research aim here is to build a CLIR system that works for a language pair with poor resources where the source language (e.g. Indonesian) has limited language resources. Our Indonesian-Japanese CLIR system employs the existing Japanese IR system, and we focus our research on the Indonesian-Japanese query translation. There are two problems in our limited resource query translation: the OOV problem and the translation ambiguity. The OOV problem is handled using target language's resources (English-Japanese dictionary and Japanese proper name dictionary). The translation ambiguity is handled using a Japanese monolingual corpus in our translation filtering. We select the final translation set using the mutual information score and the TF×IDF score. The result on NTCIR 3 (NII-NACSIS Test Collection for IR Systems) Web Retrieval Task shows that the translation method achieved a higher IR score than the transitive machine translation (using Kataku (Indonesian-English) and Babelfish/ Excite (English-Japanese) engine) result. The best result achieved about 49% of the monolingual retrieval.

1 Introductions

Due to the various languages used by different nations in the world, the CLIR has been an interesting research topic. For language pair with a rich language resource, the translation in the CLIR can be done with a bilingual dictionary - based direct translation, machine translation - or a parallel corpus - based translation. For a rare language pair, there is an attempt to use a pivot language (usually English), known as transitive translation, because there is no ample bilingual dictionary or machine translation system available. Some studies have been done in the field of transitive translation using bilingual dictionaries in the CLIR system such as [Ballesteros 2000; Gollins and Sanderson 2001]. Ballesteros [2000] translated Spanish queries into French with English as the interlingua. Ballesteros used Collins Spanish-English and English-French dictionaries. Gollins and Sanderson [2001] translated German queries into English using two pivot languages (Spanish and Dutch). Gollins used the Euro Wordnet as a data resource. To our knowledge, no CLIR is available with transitive translation for a source language with poor data resources such as Indonesian.

Translation using a bilingual dictionary usually provides many translation alternatives only a few of which are appropriate. A transitive translation gives more translation alternatives than a direct translation. In order to select the most appropriate translation, a monolingual corpus can be used to select the best translation. Ballesteros and Croft [1998] used an English corpus to select some English translation based on Spanish-English translation and analyzed the co-occurrence frequencies to disambiguate phrase translations. The occurrence score is called the *em* score. Each set is ranked by *em* score, and the highest ranking set is taken as the final translation. Gao et al. [2001] used a Chinese corpus to select the best English-Chinese translation set. It modified the EMMI weighting measure to calculate the term coherence score. Qu et al. [2002] selected the best Spanish-English and Chinese-English translation using an English corpus. The coherence score calculation was based on 1) web page count; 2) retrieval score; and 3) mutual information score. Mirna [2001] translated Indonesian into English and used an English monolingual corpus to select the best translation, employing a term similarity score based on the Dice similarity coefficient. Federico and Bertoldi [2002] combined the N-best translation based on an HMM model of a query translation pair and relevant document probability of the input word to rank Italian documents retrieved by English query. Kishida and Kando [2004], used all terms to retrieve a document in order to obtain the best term combination and chose the most frequent term in

Proceedings of the Workshop on How Can Computational Linguistics Improve Information Retrieval?, pages 1–8,
Sydney, July 2006. ©2006 Association for Computational Linguistics

each term translation set that appears in the top ranked document.

In our poor resource language – Japanese CLIR where we select Indonesian as the source language with limited resource, we calculate the mutual information score for each Japanese translation combination, using a Japanese monolingual corpus. After that, we select one translation combination with the highest TF×IDF score obtained from the Japanese IR engine.

By our experiments on Indonesian-Japanese CLIR, we would like to show how easy it is to build a CLIR for a restricted language resource. By using only an Indonesian (as the source language) – English dictionary we are able to retrieve Japanese documents with 41% of the performance achieved by the monolingual Japanese IR system.

The rest of the paper is organized as follows: Section 2 presents an overview of an Indonesian query sentence; Section 3 discusses the method used for our Indonesian-Japanese CLIR; Section 4 describes the comparison methods, and Section 5 presents our experimental data and the results.

2 Indonesian Query Sentence

Indonesian is the official language in Indonesia. The language is understood by people in Indonesia, Malaysia, and Brunei. The Indonesian language family is Malayo-Polynesian (Austronesian), which extends across the islands of Southeast Asia and the Pacific [Wikipedia]. Indonesian is not related to either English or Japanese.

Unlike other languages used in Indonesia such as Javanese, Sundanese and Balinese that use their own scripts, Indonesian uses the familiar Roman script. It uses only 26 letters as in the English alphabet. A transliteration module is not needed to translate an Indonesian sentence.

Indonesian language does not have declensions or conjugations. The basic sentence order is Subject-Verb-Object. Verbs are not inflected for person or number. There are no tenses. Tense is denoted by the time adverb or some other tense indicators. The time adverb can be placed at the front or end of the sentence.

A rather complex characteristic of the Indonesian language is that it is an agglutinave language. Words in Indonesian, usually verbs, can be attached by many prefixes or suffixes. Affixes used in the Indonesian language include [Kosasih 2003] me(n)-, ber-, di-, ter-, pe(n)-, per-, se-, ke-, -el-, -em-, -er-, -kan, -i, -nya, -an, me(n)-kan, di-kan, memper-i, diper-i, ke-an, pe(n)-an, per-an, ber-an, ber-kan, se-nya. Words with different affixes might have uniform or different translation. Examples of different word translation are "membaca" and "pembaca", which are translated into "read" and "reader", respectively. Examples of same word translation are the words "baca" and "bacakan", which are both translated into "read" in English. Other examples are the words "membaca" and "dibaca", which are translated into "read" and "being read", respectively. By using a stop word elimination, the translation result of "membaca" and "dibaca" will give the same English translation, "read".

An Indonesian dictionary usually contains words with affixes (that have different translations) and base words. For example, "se-nya" affix declares a "most possible" pattern, such as "sebanyak-banyaknya" (as much as possible), "sesedikit-sedikitnya" (less possible), "sehitam-sehitamnya" (as black as possible). This affix can be attached to many adjectives with the same meaning pattern. Therefore, words with "se-nya" affix are usually not included in an Indonesian dictionary.

Query 1 Saya ingin mengetahui siapa yang telah menjadi peraih *Academy Awards* beberapa generasi secara berturut-turut (I want to know who have been the recipients of successive generations of *Academy Awards*)
Query 2 Temukan buku-buku yang mengulas tentang novel yang ditulis oleh *Miyabe Miyuki* (Find book reviews of novels written by *Miyabe Miyuki*)

Figure 1. Indonesian Query Examples

Indonesian sentences usually consist of native (Indonesian) words and borrowed words. The two query examples in Figure 1 contain borrowed words. The first query contains "Academy Awards", which is borrowed from the English language. The second query contains "Miyabe Miyuki", which is transliterated from Japanese. To obtain a good translation, the query translation in our system must be able to translate those words, the Indonesian (native) words and the borrowed words. Problems that occur in a query translation here include OOV words and translation ambiguity.

3 Indonesian - Japanese Query Translation System

Indonesian-Japanese query translation is a component of the Indonesian-Japanese CLIR. The query translation system aims to translate an

Indonesian query sentence(s) into a Japanese keyword list. The Japanese keyword list is then executed in the Japanese IR system to retrieve the relevant document. The schema of the Indonesian-Japanese query translation system can be seen in Figure 2.

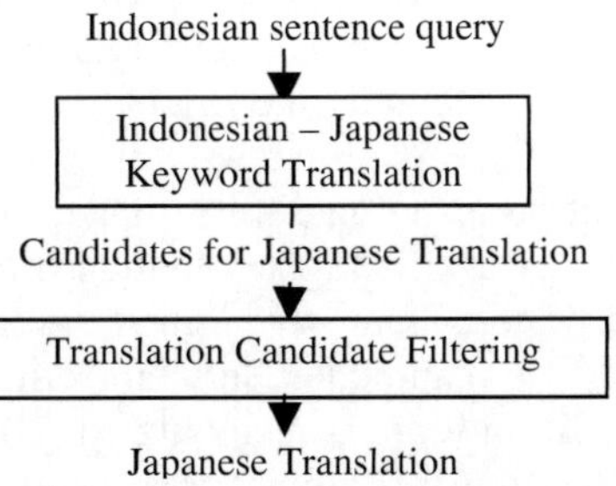

Figure 2. Indonesian-Japanese Query Translation Schema

The query translation system consists of 2 subsystems: the keyword translation and translation candidate filtering. The keyword translation system seeks to obtain Japanese translation candidates for an Indonesian query sentence. The translation candidate filtering aims to select the most appropriate translation among all Japanese translation alternatives. The filtering result is used as the input for the Japanese IR system. The keyword translation and translation filtering process is described in the next section.

3.1 Indonesian – Japanese Key Word Translation Process

The keyword translation system is a process used to translate Indonesian keywords into Japanese keywords. In this research, we do transitive translation using bilingual dictionaries as the proposed method. Other approaches such as direct translation or machine translation are employed for the comparison method. The schema of our keyword transitive translation using bilingual dictionaries is shown in Figure 3.

The keyword translation process consists of native (Indonesian) word translation and borrowed word translation. The native words are translated using Indonesian-English and English-Japanese dictionaries. Because the Indonesian tag parser is not available, we do the translation on a single word and consecutive pair of words that exist as a single term in the Indonesian-English dictionary. As mentioned in the previous section dealing with affix combination in Indonesian language, not all words with the affix combination are recorded in an Indonesian dictionary. Therefore, if a search does not reveal the exact word, it will search for other words that are the basic term of the query word or have the same basic term. For example, the Indonesian word, "munculnya" (come out), has a basic term "muncul" with the postfix "-nya". Here, the term "munculnya" is not available in the dictionary. Therefore, the searching will take "muncul" as the matching word with "munculnya" and give the English translation for "muncul" such as "come out" as its translation result.

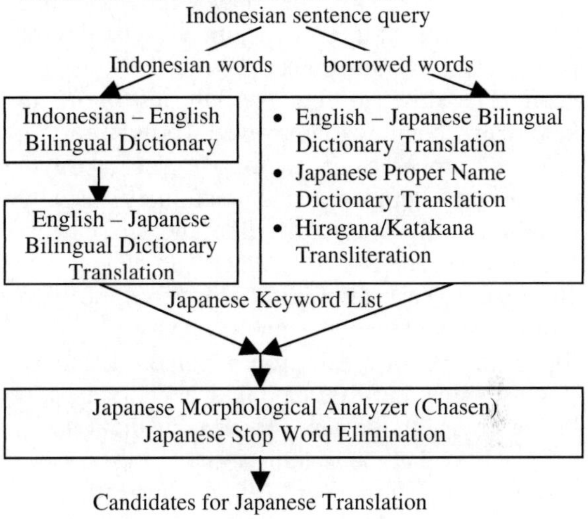

Figure 3. Indonesian-Japanese Keyword Translation Schema

In Indonesian, a noun phrase has the reverse word position of that in English. For example, "ozone hole" is translated as "lubang ozon" (ozone=ozon, hole=lubang) in Indonesian. Therefore, in English translation, besides word-by-word translation, we also search for the reversed English word pair as a single term in an English-Japanese dictionary. This strategy reduces the number of translation alternatives.

The borrowed words are translated using an English-Japanese dictionary. The English-Japanese dictionary is used because most of the borrowed words in our query translation system come from English. Examples of borrowed words in our query are "Academy Awards", "Aurora", "Tang", "baseball", "Plum", "taping", and "Kubrick".

Even though using an English-Japanese dictionary may help with accurate translation of words, but there are some proper names which can not be translated by this dictionary, such as "Miyabe Miyuki", "Miyazaki Hayao", "Honjo Manami", etc. These proper names come from Japanese words which are romanized. In the Japanese language, these proper names might be written in one of the following scripts: kanji (Chinese character), hiragana, katakana and romaji (roman alphabet). One alphabet word can be transliterated into more than one Japanese words. For example, "Miyabe" can be transliterated into 宮部, 宮辺, みやべ or ミヤベ. 宮部 and 宮辺 are written in kanji, みやべ is written in hiragana, and ミヤベ is written in katakana. For hiragana and katakana script, the borrowed word is translated by using a pair list between hiragana or katakana and its roman alphabet. These systems have a one-to-one correspondence for pronunciation (syllables or phonemes), something that can not be done for kanji. Therefore, to find the Japanese word in kanji corresponding to borrowed words, we use a Japanese proper name dictionary. Each term in the original proper name dictionary usually consists of two words, the first and last names. For a wider selection of translation candidates, we separate each term with two words into two terms. Even though the input word can not be found in the original proper name dictionary (family name and first name), a match may still be possible with the new proper name dictionary.

Each of the above translation processes also involves the stop word elimination process, which aims to delete stop words or words that do not have significant meaning in the documents retrieved. The stop word elimination is done at every language step. First, Indonesian stop word elimination is applied to a Indonesian query sentence to obtain Indonesian keywords. Second, English stop word elimination is applied before English keywords are translated into Japanese keywords. Finally, Japanese stop word elimination is done after the Japanese keywords are morphologically analyzed by Chasen (http://chasen.naist.jp/hiki/ChaSen).

The keyword transitive translation is used in 2 systems: 1) transitive translation to translate all words in the query, and 2) transitive translation to translate OOV (Indonesian) words from direct translation using an Indonesian-Japanese dictionary. We label the first method as the transitive translation using bilingual dictionary and the second method as the combined translation (direct-transitive).

3.2 Candidate Filtering Process

The keyword transitive translation results in many more translation candidates than the direct translation result. The candidates have a translation ambiguity problem which will be handled by our Japanese translation candidate filtering process, which seeks to select the most appropriate translation among the Japanese translation candidates. In order to select the best Japanese translation, rather than choosing only the highest TF× IDF score or only the highest mutual information score among all sets, we combine both scores. The procedure is as follows:

1. Calculate the mutual information score for all term sets. To avoid calculation of all term sets, we calculate the mutual information score iteratively. First we calculate it for 2 translation candidate sets. Then we select 100 sets with the highest mutual information score. These sets are joined with the 3rd translation candidate sets and the mutual information score is recalculated. This step is repeated until all translation candidate sets are covered.
   For a word set, the mutual information score is shown in Equation 1.
   $$I(t_1 \ldots t_n) = \sum_{i=1}^{n-1}\sum_{j=i+1}^{n} I(t_i;t_j) = \sum_{i=1}^{n-1}\sum_{j=i+1}^{n} \frac{\log P(t_i,t_j)}{\log P(t_i).\log P(t_j)} \qquad (1)$$
   $I(t_1 \ldots t_n)$ means the mutual information for a set of words t_1, t_2,…t_n. $I(t_i,t_j)$ means the mutual information between two words (t_i,t_j). Here, for a zero frequency word, it will have no impact on the mutual information score of a word set.
2. Select 5 sets with highest mutual information score and execute them into the IR engine in order to obtain the TF× IDF scores. The TF × IDF score used here is the relevance score between the document and the query (Equation (2) from Fujii and Ishikawa [2003]).
   $$\sum_t \left(\frac{TF_{t,i}}{\frac{DL_i}{avglen} + TF_{t,i}} . \log \frac{N}{DF_t} \right) \qquad (2)$$
   $TF_{t,i}$ denotes the frequency of term t appearing in document i. DF_t denotes the number of documents containing term t. N indicates the total number of documents in the collection. DL_i denotes the length of document i (i.e., the number of characters contained in i), and avglen the average length of documents in the collection.
3. Select the term set with the highest mutual information score among 3 top TF× IDF scores

Figure 4 shows an example of the keyword selection process after completion of the keyword translation process. The translation combination and set rankings are for all words (4 translation sets) in the query. Actually, the translation combinations and sets for the query example are also ranked for 2 and 3 translation sets. All resulting sets (ranked by its mutual information score) are executed in the IR system in order to obtain the TF× IDF score. The final query chosen is the one with the highest TF× IDF score.

Query:
Saya ingin mengetahui metode untuk belajar bagaimana menari salsa (= I wanted to know the method of studying how to dance the salsa)

Keyword Selection:
Metode (method), belajar (to learn, to study, to take up), menari (dance), salsa

Japanese Keyword:
Metode: 規則正し, 筋道, 秩序, 方法
Belajar: 調べる, 勉強, 研究, 学ぶ, 調査, 検討, 書斎, 知る, わかる, 暗記, 覚える, 確認, 習う, 突きとめる
Menari: 舞踊, ダンス, パーティー, バレエ, 舞う, 踊る, 踊ら
Salsa: サルサ

Translation Combination:
(規則正し, 調べる, 舞踊, サルサ)
(筋道, 調べる, 舞踊, サルサ)
(秩序, 調べる, 舞踊, サルサ), etc

Rank sets based on Mutual Information Score:
1. (秩序, 知る, 踊る, サルサ)
2. (秩序, 研究, 踊る, サルサ)
3. (方法, わかる, ダンス, サルサ)
4. (方法, 覚える, ダンス, サルサ)
5. (秩序, わかる, 踊る, サルサ)

Select query with highest TF×IDF score
方法. わかる. ダンス. サルサ

Figure 4. Illustration of Translation Filtering Method

4 Compared Methods

In the experiment, we compare our proposed method with other translation methods. Methods for comparing Indonesian-Japanese query translation include transitive translation using MT (machine translation), direct translation using existing Indonesian-Japanese dictionary, direct translation using a built-in Indonesian-Japanese dictionary, transitive translation with English keyword selection based on mutual information taken from English corpus, and transitive translation with Japanese keyword selection based on mutual information only.

4.1 Transitive Translation using Machine Translation

The first method compared is a transitive translation using MT (machine translation). The Indonesian- Japanese transitive translation using MT has a schema similar to Indonesian-Japanese transitive translation using a bilingual dictionary. However, machine transitive translation does not use Indonesian-English and English-Japanese dictionaries. Indonesian queries are translated into English queries using an online Indonesian-English MT (Kataku engine, http://www.toggletext.com). The English translation results are then translated into Japanese using 2 online MTs (Babelfish engine, http://www.altavista.com/babelfish and Excite engine, http://www.excite.co.jp/world).

4.2 Direct Translation using Existing Indonesian-Japanese Bilingual Dictionary

The second method compared is a direct translation using an Indonesian-Japanese dictionary. This direct translation also has a schema similar to the transitive translation using bilingual dictionary (Figure 2). The difference is that in translation of an Indonesian keyword, only 1 dictionary is used, rather than using 2 dictionaries; in this case, an Indonesian-Japanese bilingual dictionary with a fewer words than the Indonesian-English and English-Japanese dictionaries.

4.3 Direct Translation using Built-in Indonesian-Japanese Dictionary

We also compare the transitive translation results with the direct translation using a built-in Indonesian-Japanese dictionary. The Indonesian-Japanese dictionary is built from Indonesian-English, English-Japanese and Japanese-English dictionaries using "one-time inverse consultation" such as in Tanaka and Umemura [1998]. The matching process is similar with that in query translation. A Japanese translation is searched for an English translation (from every Indonesian term in Indonesian-English dictionary) as a term in the Japanese-English dictionary. If no match can be found, the English terms will be normalized by eliminating certain stop words ("to", "a", "an", "the", "to be", "kind of"). These normalized English terms will be checked again in the Japanese-English dictionary. For every Japanese translation, a "one-time inverse consultation" is calculated. If the score is more than one (for more than one English term), then it is accepted as an Indonesian-Japanese pair. If not, the WordNet is used to find its synonym and recalculate the "one-time inverse consultation" score so as to compensate for the poor quality of Indonesian-English dictionary (29054 words).

5 Experiments

5.1 Experimental Data

We measure our query translation performance by the IR score achieved by a CLIR system because CLIR is a real application and includes the performance of key word expansion. For this, we do not use word translation accuracy, as for the CLIR, since a one-to-one translation rate is not suitable, given there are so many semantically equivalent words.

Our CLIR experiments are conducted on NTCIR-3 Web Retrieval Task data (100 Gb Japanese documents), in which the Japanese queries and translated English queries were prepared. The Indonesian queries (47 queries) are manually translated from English queries. The 47 queries contain 528 Indonesian words (225 are not stop words), 35 English borrowed words, and 16 transliterated Japanese words (proper nouns). The IR system (Fujii and Ishikawa [2003]) is borrowed from Atsushi Fujii (Tsukuba University). External resources used in the query translation are listed in Table 1.

Table 1. External Resource List

Resource	Description
KEBI	Indonesian-English dictionary, 29,054 words
Eijirou	English-Japanese dictionary, 556,237 words
Kmsmini2000	Indonesian-Japanese dictionary, 14,823 words
ToggleText Kataku	Indonesian-English machine translation
Excite	English-Japanese machine translation
Babelfish	English-Japanese machine translation
[Fox, 1989] and [Zu et al., 2004]	English stop words (are also translated into Indonesian stop words)
Chasen	Japanese morphological analyzer
Jinmei Jisho	Japanese proper name dictionary, 61,629 words
Mainichi Shinbun & Online Yomiuri Shinbun	Japanese newspaper corpus

5.2 Experimental Result

In the experiments, we compare the IR score of each translation method. The IR scores shown in this section are in Mean Average Precision (MAP) scores. The evaluation metrics is referred to [Fujii and Ishikawa 2003b]. Each query group has 4 MAP scores: RL (highly relevant document as correct answer with hyperlink information used), RC (highly relevant document as correct answer), PL (partially relevant document as correct answer with hyperlink information used), and PC (partially relevant document as correct answer). The documents hyperlinked from retrieved documents are used for relevance assessment.

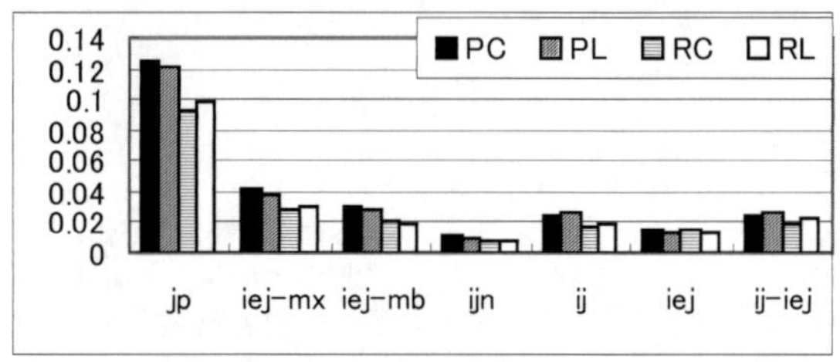

Figure 5. Baseline Indonesian-Japanese CLIR

Figure 5 shows the IR scores of queries translated using basic translation methods such as the bilingual dictionary or machine translation, without any enhanced process. The labels used in Figure 5 are:

- jp (monolingual translation), where "jp" denotes Japanese query
- iej (transitive translation using bilingual dictionary), where "i", "e", "j" denote Indonesian, English and Japanese, respectively,
- iej-mx (transitive machine translation using Kataku and Excite engines), where "m" denotes machine translation,
- iej-mb (transitive machine translation using Kataku and Babelfish engines),
- ijn (direct translation using the built in Indonesian-Japanese dictionary),
- ij (direct translation using Indonesian-Japanese dictionary),
- ij-iej (combination of direct (ij) and transitive (iej) translation using bilingual dictionary).

The highest CLIR score in the baseline translation (without the enhancement process) achieves 30% of the performance achieved by the monolingual IR (jp).

IR results in Figure 6 shows that OOV translation does improve the retrieval result. Here, our proposed methods (iej and ij-iej) achieve lower score than the comparison methods.

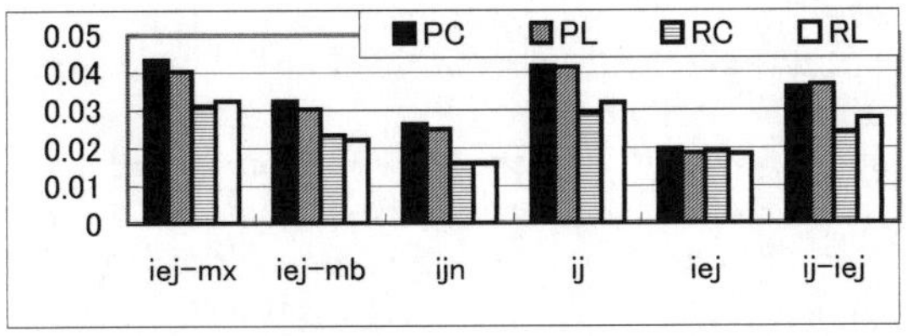

Figure 6. Indonesian-Japanese CLIR with OOV Translation

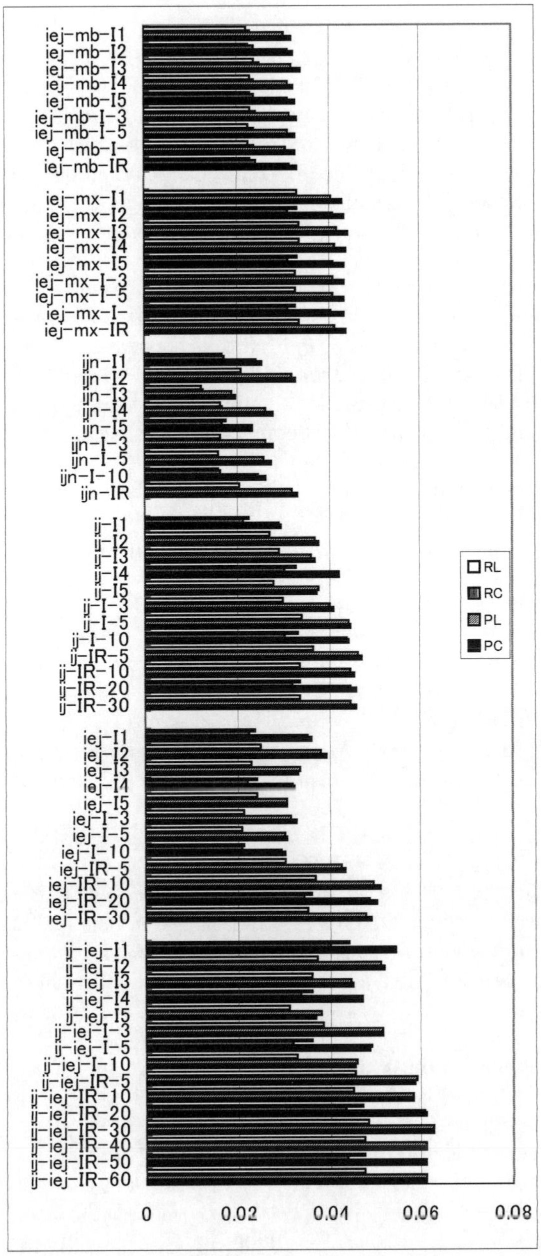

Figure 7. Indonesian-Japanese CLIR with OOV Translation and Keyword Filtering

Figure 7 shows the MAP score on the proposed Indonesian-Japanese CLIR. The keyword selection description of each query label follows:

- In (n = 1 .. 5): one query candidate based on mutual information score; example: I2 means the 2nd ranked query by its mutual information score.
- I-n (n = 3,5,10): combination of the n-best query candidates based on mutual information score; example: iej-3 (disjuncture of the 3-best mutual information score candidates).
- IR: the 1-best query candidate based on combination of mutual information score and TF× IDF engine score. X in IR-X shows number of combinations. For example, IR-5 means the highest TF× IDF score among 5 highest mutual information score sets.

Figure 7 shows that the proposed filtering method yields higher IR score on the transitive translation. We achieve 41% of the performance achieved by the monolingual IR. The proposed transitive translation (iej-IR-10) improves the IR score of the baseline method of transitive translation (iej) from 0.0156 to 0.0512. The *t*-test shows that iej-IR-10 significantly increases the baseline method (iej) with a 97% confidence level, $T(68) = 1.91$, $p<0.03$. *t*-test also shows that, compared to other baseline systems, the proposed transitive translation (iej-IR-10) can significantly increase the IR score at 85% ($T(84) = 1.04$, $p<0.15$), 69% ($T(86) = 0.49$, $p<0.31$), 91% ($T(83) = 1.35$, $p<0.09$), and 93% ($T(70) = 1.49$, $p<0.07$) confidence level for iej-mb, iej-mx, ij and ij-iej, respectively. Another proposed method, a combination of direct and transitive translation (ij-iej), achieved the best IR score among all the translation methods. The proposed combination translation method (ijiej-IR-30) improves the IR score of the baseline combination translation (ij-iej) from 0.025 to 0.0629. The *t*-test showed that the proposed combination translation improves IR score of the baseline ij-iej with a 98% confidence level, $T(69) = 2.09$, $p<0.02$. Compared to other baseline systems, *t*-test shows that the proposed combination translation method (ijiej-IR-30) improves the IR score at 95% ($T(83) = 1.66$, $p<0.05$), 86% ($T(85) = 1.087$, $p<0.14$), 97%, ($T(82) = 1.91$, $p<0.03$) and 99% ($T(67) = 2.38$, $p<0.005$) confidence level for iej-mb, iej-mx, ij and iej, respectively.

6 Conclusions

We present a translation method on CLIR that is suitable for language pair with poor resources, where the source language has a limited data resource. Compared to other translation methods such as transitive translation using machine translation and direct translation using bilingual dictionary (the source-target dictionary is a poor bilingual dictionary), our transitive translation and the combined translation (direct translation and transitive translation) achieve higher IR scores. The transitive translation achieves a 41% performance of the monolingual IR and the combined translation achieves a 49% performance of the monolingual IR.

The two important methods in our transitive translation are the borrowed word translation and the keyword selection method. The borrowed word approach can reduce the number of OOV from 50 words to 5 words using a pivot-target (English-Japanese) bilingual dictionary and target (Japanese) proper name dictionary. The keyword selection using the combination of mutual information score and TF×IDF score has improved the baseline transitive translation. The other important method, the combination method between transitive and direct translation using bilingual dictionaries also improves the CLIR performance.

Acknowledgements

We would like to give our appreciation to Dr. Atsushi Fujii (Tsukuba University) to allow us to use the IR Engine in our research. This work was partially supported by The 21st Century COE Program "Intelligent Human Sensing"

References

Adriani, Mirna. 2000. *Using statistical term similarity for sense disambiguation in cross language information retrieval.* Information Retrieval: 67-78.

Agency for The Assessment and Application of Technology: KEBI (Kamus Elektronik Bahasa Indonesia). http://nlp.aia.bppt.go.id/kebi/. Last access: February 2004.

Babelfish English-Japanese Online Machine Translation. http://www.altavista.com/babelfish/. Last access: April 2004.

Ballesteros, Lisa A. and W. Bruce Croft. 1998. *Resolving ambiguity for cross-language retrieval.* ACM Sigir.

Ballesteros, Lisa A. 2000. *Cross Language Retrieval via Transitive Translation.* Advances in Information Retrieval: 203-230. Kluwer Academic Publisher.

Chasen. http://chasen.naist.jp/hiki/ChaSen/. Last access: February 2004.

Chen, Kuang-hua, et,al. 2003. *Overview of CLIR Task at the Third NTCIR Workshop.* Proceedings of the Third NTCIR Workshop.

Excite English-Japanese Online Machine Translation. http://www.excite.co.jp/world/. Last access: April 2004.

Federico, M. and N. Bertoldi. 2002. *Statistical cross language information retrieval using n-best query translations.* Proc. Of 25th International ACM Sigir.

Fox, Christopher. 1989. *A stop list for general text.* ACM Sigir, Vol 24:19-21, Issue 2 Fall 89/Winter 90.

Fujii, Atsushi and Tetsuya Ishikawa. 2003. *NTCIR-3 cross-language IR experiments at ULIS.* Proc. Of the Third NTCIR Workshop.

Fujii, Atsushi and Katunobu Itou. 2003. *Building a test collection for speech driven web retrieval.* Proceedings of the 8th European Conference on Speech Communication and Technology.

Gao, Jianfeng, et, al. 2001. *Improving query translation for cross-language information retrieval using statistical model.* Proc. Sigir.

Gollins, Tim and Mark Sanderson. 2001. *Improving cross language information retrieval with triangulated translation.* Proc. Sigir.

ToggleText, Kataku Automatic Translation System. http://www.toggletext.com/kataku_trial.php. Last access: May 2004.

Information Retrieval Resources for Bahasia Indonesia. Informatics Institute, University of Amsterdam. http://ilps.science.uva.nl/Resources/. Last access: Jan 2005.

Kishida, Kazuaki and Noriko Kando. 2004. *Two-stage refinement of query translation in a pivot language approach to cross-lingual information retrieval: An experiment at CLEF 2003.* CLEF 2003, LNCS 3237: 253-262.

Kosasih, E. 2003. *Kompetensi Ketatabahasaan dan Kesusastraan, Cermat Berbahasa Indonesia.* Yrama Widya.

Mainichi Shinbun CD-Rom data sets 1993-1995, Nichigai Associates Co., 1994-1996.

Michibata, H., ed.: Eijirou, Alc. Last access:2002.

Qu, Yan and G. Grefenstette, D. A. Evans. 2002. *Resolving translation ambiguity using monolingual corpora.* Advanced in Cross-Language Information Retrieval, vol. 2785 of LNCS: 223-241. Springer Verlag.

Sanggar Bahasa Indonesia Proyek: Kmsmini2000. http://ml.ryu.titech.ac.jp/~indonesia/tokodai/dokumen/ kamusjpina.pdf. Last access: May 2004.

Tanaka, Kumiko and Kyoji Umemura. *Construction of a bilingual dictionary intermediated by a third language.* COLING 1994, pages 297-303, Kyoto.

Wikipedia on Indonesian Language. http://en.wikipedia.org/wiki/ Indonesian_language. Last access: May 2005.

WordNet. http://wordnet.princeton.edu/. Last access: February 2004.

Zu, Guowei, et, al. 2004. *Automatic Text Classification Techniques.* IEEJ Trans EIS, Vol. 124, No. 3.

Hybrid Systems for Information Extraction and Question Answering

Rodolfo Delmonte
Ca' Bembo, San Trovaso 1075
Università "Ca Foscari"
30123 - VENEZIA
Tel. 39-041-2345717/12 - Fax. 39-041-2345703
E-mail: delmont@unive.it - website: project.cgm.unive.it

Abstract

Information Extraction, Summarization and Question Answering all manipulate natural language texts and should benefit from the use of NLP techniques. Statistical techniques have till now outperformed symbolic processing of unrestricted text. However, Information Extraction and Question Answering require by far more accurate results of what is currently produced by Bag-Of-Words approaches. Besides, we see that such tasks as Semantic Evaluation of Text Entailment or Similarity – as required by the RTE Challenge, impose a much stricter performance in semantic terms to tell true from false pairs. We will speak in favour of a hybrid system, a combination of statistical and symbolic processing with reference to a specific problem, that of Anaphora Resolution which looms large and deep in text processing.

1. Introduction

Although full syntactic and semantic analysis of open-domain natural language text is beyond current technology, a number of papers have been recently published [1,2,3] showing that, by using probabilistic or symbolic methods, it is possible to obtain dependency-based representations of unlimited texts with good recall and precision. Consequently, we believe it should be possible to augment the manual-annotation-based approach with automatically built annotations by extracting a limited subset of semantic relations from unstructured text. In short, shallow/partial text understanding on the level of semantic relations, an extended label including Predicate-Argument Structures and other syntactically and semantically derivable head modifiers and adjuncts. This approach is promising because it attempts to address the well-known shortcomings of standard "bag-of-words" (BOWs) information retrieval/extraction techniques without requiring manual intervention: it develops current NLP technologies which make heavy use of statistically and FSA based approaches to syntactic parsing.

GETARUNS [4,5,6], a text understanding system (TUS), developed in collaboration between the University of Venice and the University of Parma, can perform semantic analysis on the basis of syntactic parsing and, after performing anaphora resolution, builds a quasi logical form with flat indexed Augmented Dependency Structures (ADSs). In addition, it uses a centering algorithm to individuate the topics or discourse centers which are weighted on the basis of a relevance score. This logical form can then be used to individuate the best sentence candidates to answer queries or provide appropriate information.

This paper is organized as follows: in section 2 below we discuss why deep linguistic processing is needed in Information Retrieval and Information Extraction; in section 3 we present GETARUNS, the NLP system and the Upper Module of GETARUNS; in section 4 we describe two experiments with state-of-the-art benchmark corpora.

2 Ternary Expressions as Predicate-Argument Structures

Researchers like Lin, Katz and Litkowski have started to work in the direction of using NLP to populate a database of RDFs, thus creating the premises for the automatic creation of ontologies to be used in the IR/IE tasks. However, in no way RDFs and ternary expressions may constitute a formal tool sufficient to express the complexity of natural language texts.

RDFs are assertions about the things (people, Webpages and whatever) they predicate about by asserting that they have certain properties with certain values. If we may agree with the fact that this is natural way of dealing with data handled by computers most frequently, it also a fact that this is not equivalent as being useful for natural language. The misconception seems to be deeply embedded in the nature of RDFs as a whole: they are directly comparable to attribute-value pairs and DAGs which are also the formalism used by most recent linguistic unification-based grammars. From the logical and semantic point of view RDFs also resemble very closely first order predicate logic constructs: but we must remember that FOPL is as such insufficient to describe natural language texts.

Ternary expressions(T-expressions), <subject relation object>.

Certain other parameters (adjectives, possessive nouns, prepositional phrases, etc.) are used to create additional T-expressions in which prepositions and several special words may serve as relations. For instance, the following simple sentence

(1) Bill surprised Hillary with his answer

Proceedings of the Workshop on How Can Computational Linguistics Improve Information Retrieval?, pages 9–16,
Sydney, July 2006.

will produce two T-expressions:

(2) <<Bill surprise Hillary> with answer>
<answer related-to Bill>

In Litkowski's system the key step in their question-answering prototype was the analysis of the parse trees to extract semantic relation triples and populate the databases used to answer the question. A semantic relation triple consists of a discourse entity, a semantic relation which characterizes the entity's role in the sentence, and a governing word to which the entity stands in the semantic relation. The semantic relations in which entities participate are intended to capture the semantic roles of the entities, as generally understood in linguistics. This includes such roles as agent, theme, location, manner, modifier, purpose, and time. Surrogate place holders included are "SUBJ," "OBJ", "TIME," "NUM," "ADJMOD," and the prepositions heading prepositional phrases. The governing word was generally the word in the sentence that the discourse entity stood in relation to. For "SUBJ," "OBJ," and "TIME," this was generally the main verb of the sentence. For prepositions, the governing word was generally the noun or verb that the prepositional phrase modified. For the adjectives and numbers, the governing word was generally the noun that was modified.

2.1 Ternary Expressions are better than the BOWs approach, but…

People working advocating the supremacy of the Tes approach were reacting against the Bag of Words approach of IR/IE in which words were wrongly regarded to be entertaining a meaningful relation simply on the basis of topological criteria: normally the distance criteria or the more or less proximity between the words to be related. Intervening words might have already been discarded from the input text on the basis of stopword filtering. Stopwords list include all grammatical close type words of the language considered useless for the main purpose of IR/IE practitioners seen that they cannot be used to denote concepts. Stopwords constitute what is usually regarded the noisy part of the channel in information theory. However, it is just because the redundancy of the information channel is guaranteed by the presence of grammatical words that the message gets appropriately computed by the subject of the communication process, i.e. human beings. Besides, entropy is not to be computed in terms of number of words or letters of the alphabet, but in number of semantic and syntactic relation entertained by open class words (nouns, verbs, adjectives, adverbials) basically by virtue of closed class words. Redundancy should then be computed on the basis of the ambiguity intervening when enumerating those relations, a very hard task to accomplish which has never been attemped yet, at least to my knowledge.
What people working with TEs noted was just the problem of encoding relations appropriately, at least some of these relations. The IR/IE BOWs approach suffers (at least) from Reversible Arguments Problem (see [7])
- What do frogs eat? vs What eats frogs?
The verb "eat" entertains asymmetrical relations with its SUBJect and its OBJect: in one case we talk of the "eater", the SUBJect and in another case of the "eatee", the OBJect. Other similar problems occur with TEs when the two elements of the relation have the same head, as in:
-The president of Russia visited the president of China. Who visited the president?
The question will not be properly answered in lack of some clarification dialogue intervening, but the corresponding TEs should have more structure to be able to represent the internal relations of the two presidents. The asymmetry of relation in transitive constructions involving verbs of accomplishments and achievements (or simply world-changing events) is however further complicated by a number of structural problems which are typically found in most languages of the world, the first one and most common being Passive constructions:
i.John killed Tom.
ii.Tom was killed by a man.
Who killed the man?
Answer to the question would be answered by "John" in case the information available was represented by sentence in i., but it would be answered by "Tom" in case the information available was represented by sentence ii. Obviously this would happen only in lack of sufficient NLP elaboration: a too shallow approach would not be able to capture presence of a passive structure. We are here referring to "Chunk"-based approaches those in which the object of computation is constituted by the creation of Noun Phrases and no attempt is made to compute clause-level structure.
There is a certain number of other similar structure in texts which must be regarded as inducing into the same type of miscomputation: i.e. taking the surface order of NPs as indicating the deep intended meaning. In all of the following constructions the surface subject is on the contrary the deep object thus the Affected Theme or argument that suffers the effects of the action expressed by the governing verb rather than the Agent:

Inchoatized structures; Ergativized structures; Impersonal structures

Other important and typical structures which constitute problematic cases for a surface chunks based TEs approach to text computation are the following ones in which one of the arguments is missing and Control should be applied by a governing NP, they are called in one definition Open Predicative structures and they are

Relative clauses; Fronted Adjectival adjunct clauses; Infinitive clauses; Fronted Participial clauses,; Gerundive Clauses; Elliptical Clauses; Coordinate constructions

In addition to that there is one further problem and is definable as the Factuality Prejudice: by collecting keywords and TEs people apply a Factuality Presupposition to the text they are mining: they believe that all terms being recovered by the search represent real facts. This is however not true and the problem is related to the possibility to detect in texts the presence of such semantic indicators as those listed here below:

Negation; Quantification; Opaque contexts (wish, want); Future, Subjunctive Mode; Modality; Conditionals

Finally there is a discourse related problem and is the **Anaphora Resolution** problem which is the hardest to be tackled by NLP: it is a fact that anaphoric relations are the building blocks of cohesiveness and coherence in texts. Whenever an anaphoric link is missed one relation will be assigned to a wrong referring expression thus presumably jeopardising the possibility to answer a related question appropriately. This is we believe the most relevant topic to be put forward in favour of the need to have symbolic computational linguistic processing (besides statistical processing).

3 GETARUNS – the NLUS

GETARUN, the System for Natural Language Understanding, produces a semantic representation in xml format, in which each sentence of the input text is divided up into predicate-argument structures where arguments and adjuncts are related to their appropriate head. Consider now a simple sentence like the following:
(1) John went into a restaurant
GETARUNS represents this sentence in different manners according to whether it is operating in Complete or in Shallow modality. In turn the operating modality is determined by its ability to compute the current text: in case of failure the system will switch automatically from Complete to Partial/Shallow modality.
The system will produce a representation inspired by Situation Semantics[14] where reality is represented in Situations which are collections of Facts: in turn facts are made up of Infons which are information units characterised as follows:

Infon(Index,
Relation(Property),
List of Arguments - with Semantic Roles,
Polarity - 1 affirmative, 0 negation,
Temporal Location Index,
Spatial Location Index)

In addition each Argument has a semantic identifier which is unique in the Discourse Model and is used to individuate the entity uniquely. Also propositional facts have semantic identifiers assigned, thus constituting second level ontological objects. They may be "quantified" over by temporal representations but also by discourse level operators, like subordinating conjunctions and a performative operator if needed. Negation on the contrary is expressed in each fact.
In case of failure at the Complete level, the system will switch to Partial and the representation will be deprived of its temporal and spatial location information. In the current version of the system, we use Complete modality for tasks which involve short texts (like the students summaries and text understanding queries), where text analyses may be supervisioned and updates to the grammar and/or the lexicon may be needed. For unlimited text from the web we only use partial modality. Evaluation of the two modalities are reported in a section below.

3.1 The Parser and the Discourse Model

As said above, the query building process needs an ontology which is created from the translation of the Discourse Model built by GETARUNS in its Complete/Partial Representation. GETARUNS, is equipped with three main modules: a lower module for parsing where sentence strategies are implemented; a middle module for semantic interpretation and discourse model construction which is cast into Situation Semantics; and a higher module where reasoning and generation takes place. The system works in Italian and English.
Our parser is a rule-based deterministic parser in the sense that it uses a lookahead and a Well-Formed Substring Table to reduce backtracking. It also implements Finite State Automata in the task of tag disambiguation, and produces multiwords whenever lexical information allows it. In our parser we use a number of parsing strategies and graceful recovery procedures which follow a strictly parameterized approach to their definition and implementation. A shallow or partial parser is also implemented and always activated before the complete parse takes place, in order to produce the default baseline output to be used by further computation in case of total failure. In that case partial semantic mapping will take place where no Logical Form is being built and only referring expressions are asserted in the Discourse Model – but see below.

3.2 Lexical Information

The output of grammatical modules is then fed onto the Binding Module(BM) which activates an algorithm for anaphoric binding in LFG (see [13]) terms using f-structures as domains and grammatical functions as entry points into the structure. We show here below the architecture of the system. The grammar is equipped with a lexicon containing a list of 30000 wordforms derived from Penn Treebank.
However, morphological analysis for English has also been implemented and used for OOV words. The system uses a core fully specified lexicon, which contains approximately 10,000 most frequent entries of English. In addition to that, there are all lexical forms provided by a fully revised version of COMLEX. In order to take into account phrasal and adverbial verbal compound forms, we also use lexical entries made available by UPenn and TAG encoding. Their grammatical verbal syntactic codes have then been adapted to our formalism and is used to generate an approximate subcategorization scheme with an approximate aspectual class associated to it.

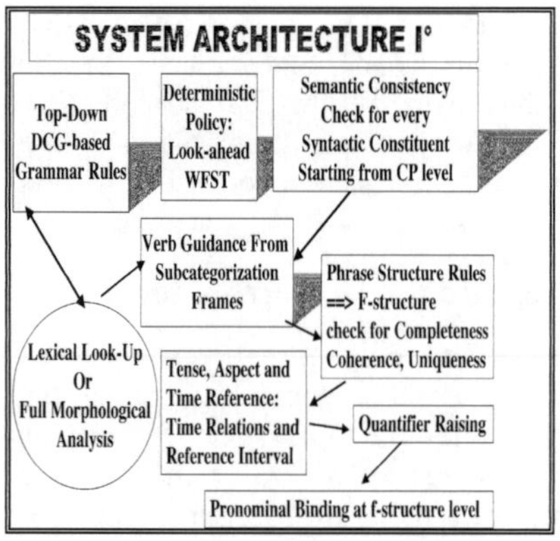

Fig. 1. GETARUNS' LFG-Based Parser

Semantic inherent features for Out of Vocabulary words, be they nouns, verbs, adjectives or adverbs, are provided by a fully revised version of WordNet – 270,000 lexical entries - in which we used 75 semantic classes similar to those provided by CoreLex. Subcategorization information and Semantic Roles are then derived from a carefully adapted version of FrameNet and VerbNet. Our "training" corpus is made up of 200,000 words and contains a number of texts taken from different genres, portions of the UPenn Treebank corpus, test-suits for grammatical relations, and sentences taken from COMLEX manual. An evaluation carried out on the Susan Corpus related GREVAL testsuite made of 500 sentences has been reported lately [12] to have achieved 90% F-measure over all major grammatical relations. We achieved a similar result with the shallow cascaded parser, limited though to only SUBJect and OBJect relations on LFG-XEROX 700 corpus.

3.3 The Upper Module

GETARUNS, as shown in Fig.2 has a linguistically-based semantic module which is used to build up the Discourse Model. Semantic processing is strongly modularized and distributed amongst a number of different submodules which take care of Spatio-Temporal Reasoning, Discourse Level Anaphora Resolution, and other subsidiary processes like Topic Hierarchy which will impinge on Relevance Scoring when creating semantic individuals. These are then asserted in the Discourse Model (hence the DM), which is then used to solve nominal coreference together with WordNet. Semantic Mapping is performed in two steps: at first a Logical Form is produced which is a structural mapping from DAGs onto of unscoped well-formed formulas. These are then turned into situational semantics informational units, infons which may become facts or sits.

In each infon, Arguments have each a semantic identifier which is unique in the DM and is used to individuate the entity. Also propositional facts have semantic identifiers assigned thus constituting second level ontological objects. They may be "quantified" over by temporal representations but also by discourse level operators, like subordinating conjunctions. Negation on the contrary is

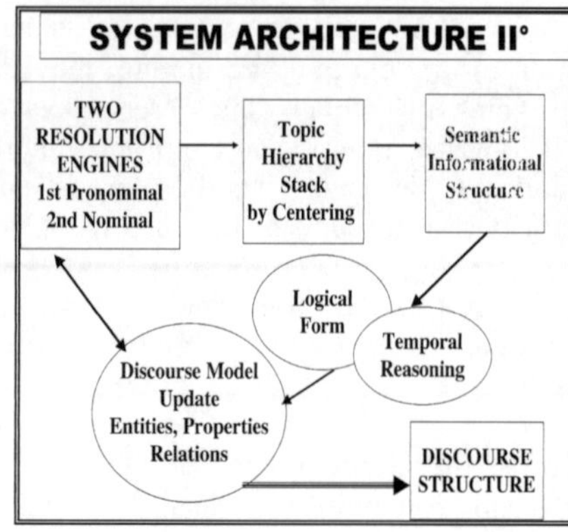

Fig. 2. GETARUNS' Discourse Level Modules

expressed in each fact. All entities and their properties are asserted in the DM with the relations in which they are involved; in turn the relations may have modifiers - sentence level adjuncts and entities may also have modifiers or attributes. Each entity has a polarity and a couple of spatiotemporal indices which are linked to main temporal and spatial locations if any exists; else they are linked to presumed time reference derived from tense and aspect computation. Entities are mapped into semantic individuals with the following ontology: on first occurrence of a referring expression it is asserted as an INDividual if it is a definite or indefinite expression; it is asserted as a CLASS if it is quantified (depending on quantifier type) or has no determiner. Special individuals are ENTs which are associated to discourse level anaphora which bind relations and their arguments. Finally, we have LOCs for main locations, both spatial and temporal. Whenever there is cardinality determined by a digit, its number is plural or it is quantified (depending on quantifier type) the referring expression is asserted as a SET. Cardinality is simply inferred in case of naked plural: in case of collective nominal expression it is set to 100, otherwise to 5. On second occurrence of the same nominal head the semantic index is recovered from the history list and the system checks whether it is the same referring expression:

- in case it is definite or indefinite with a predicative role and no attributes nor modifiers, nothing is done;
- in case it has different number - singular and the one present in the DM is a set or a class, nothing happens;
- in case it has attributes and modifiers which are different and the one present in the DM has none, nothing happens;
- in case it is quantified expression and has no cardinality, and the one present in the DM is a set or a class, again nothing happens.

In all other cases a new entity is asserted in the DM which however is also computed as being included in (a superset of) or by (a subset of) the previous entity.

The upper module of GETARUNS has been evaluated on the basis of its ability to perform anaphora resolution and to individuate referring expressions, with a corpus of 40,000 words: it achieved 74% F-measure.

4. Two experiments with GETURANS

As an example of the shallow system we discuss here below the analysis of a newspaper article which as would usually be the case has a certain number of pronominal expressions, which modify the relevance of lexical descriptions in the overall processing for the search of either "Named Entities" or simply entities individuated by common nouns. If the count is based solely on lexical lemmata and not on the presence of coreferential pronominal expressions, the results will be heavily biased and certainly wrong. Here is the text:

1.Thursday, 25th June 2001
National Parties and the Internet
by Joanna Crawford
2.A survey of how national parties used the internet as a campaigning tool during the election will brand ***their*** efforts "bleak and dispiriting" - despite the pre-campaign hype of an "e-election".
3.Researchers from Salford University studied websites from all the major parties during the general election, as well as looking at every site put up by local candidates.
4.Their conclusions - to be presented tomorrow at a special conference organised by the Institute for Public Policy Research - could influence how future political contests, including the forthcoming Euro debate, are carried out on the web.
5.The report finds that ***none*** of the major three parties allowed message boards or chat rooms for users to post their opinions on the sites.
6.***It*** states: "Parties were accused of simply engaging in online propaganda with boring content and largely ignoring interactivity."
7.The report concludes: "The new media is a way for ***them*** to get closer to the public without necessarily allowing the public to become overly familiar in return.
8.The authors - Rachel Gibson and Stephen Ward - go on to state that ***this*** may be because parties still regard the web as an electioneering tool, rather than as a democratic device.
9.They said: "Very ***few*** offered original material, or changed ***their*** sites noticeably over the course of the campaign.
10.Indeed, a large ***majority*** of local sites were really no more than static electronic brochures."
11.They dub ***this*** "rather disappointing", but praise the Liberal Democrats as "clearly the most active" with around 150 sites. The report concludes: "Parties, as with the general public, need incentives to use the technology.
12.As yet, there seems more to lose and less to gain if ***they*** make mistakes experimenting with the technology."

We highlighted pronominal expressions in bold. In a BOWs approach, the count for most relevant topics is solely based on lexical descriptions and "party, internet" are computed as the most important key-words. However, after the text has been passed by the partial semantic analysis, "researcher, author" come up as important topics.
We report here below the output of the Anaphora Resolution module: in interaction with the Discourse Model where semantic indices are asserted for each entity. Sentence numbers are taken from the text. We report Anaphora Resolution decisions: in particular in sentences where a pronoun is coreferred to an antecedent, the antecedent is set as current Main Topic and its semantic ID is used.

1. state(1, change)
topics: main:party, secondary: internet
topics(1, main, id1; secondary, id2; potential, id3)
2. state(2, continue)
topics: main:party, secondary: survey
topics(2, main, id1; secondary, id7; potential, id2)
3. state(3, retaining)
topics: main: researcher, secondary: party
topic(3, main, id18; secondary, id1; , id19)
4. Anaphora Resolution: their resolved as researcher
state(4, continue)
topics: main: researcher, secondary: contest
topics(4, main, id18; secondary, id26; potential, id27)
5. state(5, retaining)
topics: main: report, secondary: researcher
topics(5, main, id7; secondary, id18; potential, id1)
6. Anaphora Resolution: it resolved as report
state(6, continue)
topics: main: report, secondary: party
topics(6, main, id7; secondary, id1; potential, id40)
7. state(7, continue)
topics: main: report, secondary: party
topics(7, main, id7; secondary, id1; potential, id2)
8. The authors - Rachel Gibson and Stephen Ward - go on to state that this may be because parties still regard the web as an electioneering tool, rather than as a democratic device.
Anaphora Resolution: this resolved as 'discourse bound'
state(8, retaining)
topics: main: author, secondary: report
topics(8, main, id54; secondary, id7; potential, id55)
9. Anaphora Resolution: they resolved as author
state(9, continue)
topics: main: author, secondary: material
topics(9, main, id54; secondary, id61; potential, id62)
10. state(10, continue)
topics: main: author, secondary: site
topics(10, main, id54; secondary, id67; potential, id68)
11. Anaphora Resolution: this resolved as 'discourse bound'; they resolved as author
state(11, retaining)
topics: main: author, secondary: active
topics(11, main, id54; secondary, id71; potential, id72)
12. Anaphora Resolution: they resolved as party
state(12, continue)
topics: main: party, secondary: mistake
topics(12, main, id1; secondary, id78)

4.1 The First Experiment: Anaphora Resolution in Technical Manuals

We downloaded the only freely available corpus annotated with anaphoric relations, i.e. Wolverhampton's Manual Corpus made available by Prof. Ruslan Mitkov on his website. The corpus contains text from Manuals at the following address,
http://clg.wlv.ac.uk/resources/corpus.html

Text Type	Referring Exps	Coreferring Exps	Total Words
AIWA	1629	716	6818
ACCESS	1862	513	9381
PANASONIC	1263	537	4829
HINARI	673	292	2878
URBAN	453	81	2222
WINHELP	672	206	2935
CDROM	1944	279	10568
Totals	8496	2624	39631

Table 2. General data of Worlverhampton's coreference annotated corpora

Text Type	Referring Exps % W	Coreferring Exps % RE
AIWA	23.89	*43.21*
ACCESS	19.84	27.01
PANASONIC	26.15	*42.51*
HINARI	23.38	29,22
URBAN	20.38	**17.88**
WINHELP	22.89	27.14
CDROM	18.39	**14.24**
Means	21.43	30.88

Table 3. Proportion of coreferential expressions to referring expressions

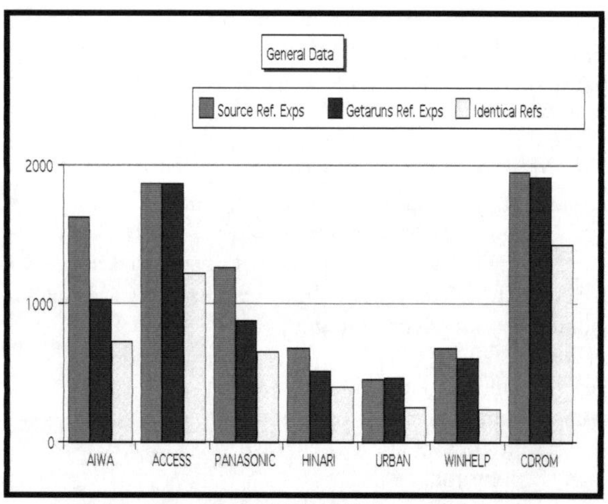

Fig. 3. Comparing GETARUNS output to WMC

We reported in Tab. 2 the general data of the Coreference Corpus. As can be easily noted, there is no direct relationship existing between the number of referring expressions and the number of coreferring expressions. We assume that the higher the number of coreferring expressions in a text the higher is the cohesion achieved. Thus the text identified as CDROM has a very small number of coreferring expressions if compared to the total number of referring expressions. The proportion of referring expressions to words and of coreferring expressions to referring expressions is reported in percent value in table 3. where the most highly cohesive texts are highlighted in italics; highly non cohesive texts are highlighted in bold:

The final results are reported in the following figure where we plot Precision and Recall for each text and then the comprehensive values.

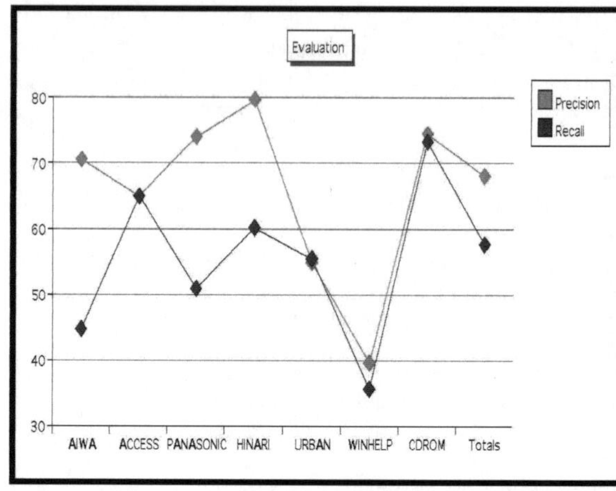

Fig. 4. Precision and Recall for the WMC

4.2 GETARUNS approach to WEB-Q/A

Totally shallow approaches when compared to ours will always be lacking sufficient information for semantic processing at propositional level: in other words, as happens with our "Partial" modality, there will be no possibility of checking for precision in producing predicate-argument structures.

Most systems would use some Word Matching algorithm to count the number of words appearing in both question and the sentence being considered after stripping stopwords: usually two words will match if they share the same morphological root after some stemming has taken place. Most QA systems presented in the literature rely on the classification of words into two classes: function and content words. They don't make use of a Discourse Model where input text has been transformed via a rigorous semantic mapping algorithm: they rather access tagged input text in order to sort best matched words, phrases or sentences according to some scoring function. It is an accepted fact that introducing or increasing the amount of linguistic knowledge over crude IR-based systems will contribute substantial improvements. In particular, systems based on simple Named-Entity identification tasks are too rigid to be able to match phrase relations constraints often involved in a natural language query.

We raise a number of objections to these approaches: first objection is the impossibility to take into account pronominal expressions, their relations and properties as belonging to the antecedent, if no head transformation has taken place during the analysis process.

Another objection comes from the treatment of the Question: it is usually the case that QA systems divide the question to be answered into two parts: the Question

Target represented by the wh- word and the rest of the sentence; otherwise the words making up the yes/no question are taken in their order, and then a match takes place in order to identify most likely answers in relation to the rest/whole of the sentence except for stopwords.
However, it is just the semantic relations that need to be captured and not just the words making up the question that matter. Some systems implemented more sophisticated methods (notably [8;9;10]) using syntactic-semantic question analysis. This involves a robust syntactic-semantic parser to analyze the question and candidate answers, and a matcher that combines word- and parse-tree-level information to identify answer passages more precisely.

4.3 A Prototype Q/A system for the web

We experimented our approach over the web using 450 factoid questions from TREC. On a first run the base system only used an off-the-shelf tagger in order to recover main verb from the query. In this way we managed to get 67% correct results, by this meaning that the correct answer was contained in the best five snippets selected by the BOWs system on the output of Google API. However, only 30% of the total correct results had the right snippet ranked in position one.
Then we applied GETARUNS shallow on the best five snippets with the intent of improving the automatic ranking of the system and have the best snippet always position as first possibility. Here below is a figure showing the main components for GETARUNS based analysis.
We will present two examples and discuss them in some detail. The questions are the following ones:
Q: Who was elected president of South Africa in 1994?
A: Nelson Mandela
Q: When was Abraham Lincoln born?
A: Lincoln was born February_12_1809
The answers produced by our system are indicated after each question. Now consider the best five snippets as filtered by the BOWs system:

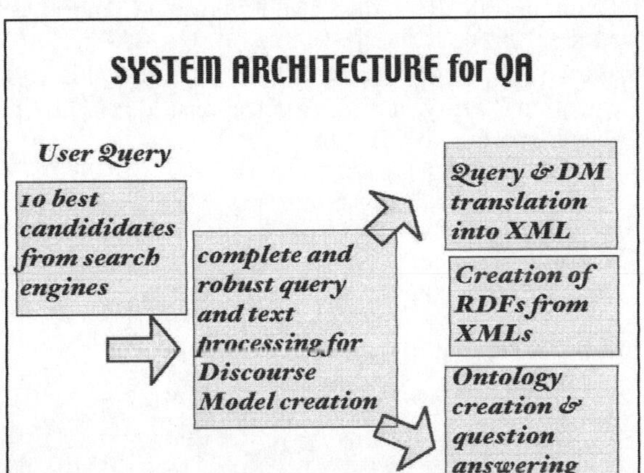

Fig. 5. System Architecture for QA

who/WP was/VBD elected/VBN president/NN of/IN south/JJ africa/NN in/IN 1994/CD
Main keywords: president south africa 1994
Verb roots: elect
Google search: elected president south africa 1994

1.On June 2, 1999, Mbeki, the pragmatic deputy president of South Africa and leader of the African National Congress, was elected president in a landslide, having already assumed many of Mandela's governing responsibilities shortly after Mandela won South Africa's first democratic election in 1994.
2.Washington ? President Bill Clinton announced yesterday a doubling in US assistance South Africa of $600-million (R2 160-million) over three years, and said his wife Hillary would attend Nelson Mandela's inauguration as the country's first black president.
3.Nelson Mandela, President of the African National Congress (ANC), casting the ballot in his country's first all-race elections, in April 1994 at Ohlange High School near Durban, South Africa.
4.Newly-elected President Nelson Mandela addressing the crowd from a balcony of the Town Hall in Pretoria, South Africa on May 10, 1994.
5.The CDF boycotted talks in King William's Town yesterday called by the South African government and the Transitional Executive Council to smooth the way for the peaceful reincorporation of the homeland into South Africa following the resignation of Oupa Gqozo as president.

Notice snippet n.1 where two presidents are present and two dates are reported for each one: however the relation "president" is only indicated for the wrong one, Mbeki and the system rejects it. The answer is collected from snippet no.4 instead. As a matter of fact, after computing the ADM, the system decides to rerank the snippets and use the contents of snippet 4 for the answer. Now the second question:

when/WRB was/VBD abraham/NN lincoln/NN born/VBN
Main keywords: abraham lincoln
Verb roots: bear
Google search: abraham lincoln born

1. Abraham Lincoln was born in a log cabin in Kentucky to Thomas and Nancy Lincoln.
2. Two months later on February 12, 1809, Abraham Lincoln was born in a one-room log cabin near the Sinking Spring.
3. Abraham Lincoln was born in a log cabin near Hodgenville, Kentucky.
4.Lincoln himself set the date of his birth at feb_ 12, 1809, though some have attempted to disprove that claim .
5. A. Lincoln (February 12, 1809 April 15, 1865) was the 16/th president of the United States of America.

In this case, snippet n.2 is selected by the system as the one containing the required information to answer the question. In both cases, the answer is built from the ADM, so it is not precisely the case that the snippets are selected for the answer: they are nonetheless reranked to make the answer available.

5. System Evaluation

After running with GETARUNS, the 450 questions recovered the whole of the original correct result 67% from first snippet.
The complete system has been tested with a set of texts derived from newspapers, narrative texts, children stories. The performance is 75% correct. However, updating and tuning of the system is required for each

new text whenever a new semantic relation is introduced by the parser and the semantics does not provide the appropriate mapping. For instance, consider the case of the constituent "holes in the tree", where the syntax produces the appropriate structure but the semantics does not map "holes" as being in a LOCATion semantic relation with "tree". In lack of such a semantic role information a dummy "MODal" will be produced which however will not generate the adequate semantic mapping in the DM and the meaning is lost.

As to the partial system, it has been used for DUC summarization contest, i.e. it has run over approximately 1 million words, including training and test sets, for a number of sentences totalling over 50K. We tested the "Partial" modality with an additional 90,000 words texts taken from the testset made available by DUC 2002 contest. On a preliminary perusal of samples of the results, we calculated 85% Precision on parsing and 70% on semantic mapping. However evaluating full results requires a manually annotated database in which all linguistic properties have been carefully decided by human annotators. In lack of such a database, we are unable to provide precise performance data. The system has also been used for the RTE Challenge and performance was over 60% correct [11].

6. Conclusions

Results reported in the experiment above have been limited to the ability of the system to cope with what has always been regarded as the toughest task for an NLP system to cope with. We have not addressed the problem of question answering for lack of space.

Would it be possible for computers the recognize the layout of a Web page, much in the same manner as a human? Much like the development of the Semantic Web itself, early efforts to integrate natural language technology with the Semantic Web will no doubt be slow and incremental. By weaving natural language into the basic fabric of the Semantic Web, we can begin to create an enormous network of knowledge easily accessible by both machines and humans alike. Furthermore, we believe that natural language querying capabilities will be a key component of any future Semantic Web system. By providing "natural" means for creating and accessing information on the Semantic Web, we can dramatically lower the barrier of entry to the Semantic Web. Natural language support gives users a whole new way of interacting with any information system, and from a knowledge engineering point of view, natural language technology divorces the majority of users from the need to understand formal ontologies. As we have tried to show in the paper, this calls for better NLP tools where a lot of effort has to be put in order to allow for complete and shallow techniques to coalesce smoothly into one single system. GETARUNS represents such a hybrid system and its performance is steadily improving.

In the future we intend to address the problem of using the database of TEs created by our system in asnswering a more extended set of natural language queries than what has been tried sofar.

References

1. Dan Klein and Christopher D. Manning: Accurate Unlexicalized Parsing. ACL, (2003) 423-430
2. D. Lin.: Dependency-based evaluation of MINIPAR. In Proceedings of the Workshop on Evaluation of Parsing Systems at LREC 1998. Granada, Spain, (1998)
3. Sleator, Daniel, and Davy Temperley: "Parsing English with a Link Grammar." Proceedings of IWPT '93, (1993)
4. Delmonte R.: Parsing Preferences and Linguistic Strategies, in *LDV-Forum - Zeitschrift fuer Computerlinguistik und Sprachtechnologie - "Communicating Agents"*, Band 17, 1,2, (2000) 56-73
5. Delmonte R.: Parsing with GETARUN, *Proc.TALN2000, 7° conférence annuel sur le TALN*, Lausanne, (2000) 133-146
6. Delmonte R., D. Bianchi: From Deep to Partial Understanding with GETARUNS, *Proc. ROMAND 2002*, Università Roma2, Roma, (2002) 57-71
7. Boris Katz, Jimmy J. Lin, Sue Felshin: The START Multimedia Information System: Current Technology and Future Directions, In Proceedings of the International Workshop on Multimedia Information Systems (MIS 2002)
8. Hovy, E., U. Hermjakob, & C. Lin.: The Use of External Knowledge in Factoid QA. In E. M. Voorhees & D. K. Harman (eds.), *The Tenth Text Retrieval Conference (TREC 2001).* (2002) 644-652
9. Litkowski, K. C.: Syntactic Clues and Lexical Resources in Question-Answering. In E. M. Voorhees & D. K. Harman (eds.), *The Ninth Text Retrieval Conference (TREC-9).* (2001) 157-166
10. Litkowski, K. C.: CL Research Experiments in TREC-10 Question-Answering. In E. M. Voorhees & D. K. Harman (eds.), *The Tenth Text Retrieval Conference (TREC 2001).* (2002) 122-131
11. Delmonte R., Sara Tonelli, Marco Aldo Piccolino Boniforti, Antonella Bristot, Emanuele Pianta: VENSES – a Linguistically-Based System for Semantic Evaluation, RTE Challenge Workshop, Southampton, PASCAL - European Network of Excellence, (2005) 49-52
12. Delmonte R.: Evaluating GETARUNS Parser with GREVAL Test Suite, Proc. ROMAND - 20th International Conference on Computational Linguistics - COLING, University of Geneva, (2004) 32-41.
13. Bresnan J.(ed.): The Mental Representation of Grammatical Relations, MIT Press, Cambridge Mass., 1982)
14. Barwise J., J.M.Gawron, G.Plotkin, S.Tutiya(eds.): Situation Theory and its Applications, Vol.2, CSLI Lecture Notes No.26, (1991)

Extracting Key Phrases to Disambiguate Personal Name Queries in Web Search

Danushka Bollegala **Yutaka Matsuo** * **Mitsuru Ishizuka**
Graduate School of Information Science and Technology
The University of Tokyo
7-3-1, Hongo, Bunkyo-ku, Tokyo, 113-8656, Japan
danushka@mi.ci.i.u-tokyo.ac.jp
y.matsuo@aist.go.jp
ishizuka@i.u-tokyo.ac.jp

Abstract

Assume that you are looking for information about a particular person. A search engine returns many pages for that person's name. Some of these pages may be on other people with the same name. One method to reduce the ambiguity in the query and filter out the irrelevant pages, is by adding a phrase that uniquely identifies the person we are interested in from his/her namesakes. We propose an unsupervised algorithm that extracts such phrases from the Web. We represent each document by a *term-entity* model and cluster the documents using a contextual similarity metric. We evaluate the algorithm on a dataset of ambiguous names. Our method outperforms baselines, achieving over 80% accuracy and significantly reduces the ambiguity in a web search task.

1 Introduction

The Internet has grown into a collection of billions of web pages. Web search engines are important interfaces to this vast information. We send simple text queries to search engines and retrieve web pages. However, due to the ambiguities in the queries, a search engine may return a lot of irrelevant pages. In the case of personal name queries, we may receive web pages for other people with the same name (*namesakes*). For example, if we search *Google* [1] for *Jim Clark*, even among the top 100 results we find at least eight different *Jim Clarks*. The two popular namesakes; *Jim Clark* the Formula one world champion (46 pages), and *Jim Clark* the founder of Netscape (26 pages), cover the majority of the pages. What if we are interested only in the Formula one world champion and want to filter out the pages for the other *Jim Clarks*? One solution is to modify our query by including a phrase such as *Formula one* or *racing driver* with the name, *Jim Clark*.

This paper presents an automatic method to extract such phrases from the Web. We follow a three-stage approach. In the first stage we represent each document containing the ambiguous name by a *term-entity* model, as described in section 5.2. We define a contextual similarity metric based on snippets returned by a search engine, to calculate the similarity between term-entity models. In the second stage, we cluster the documents using the similarity metric. In the final stage, we select key phrases from the clusters that uniquely identify each namesake.

2 Applications

Two tasks that can readily benefit from automatically extracted key phrases to disambiguate personal names are *query suggestion* and *social network extraction*. In query suggestion (Gauch and Smith, 1991), the search engine returns a set of phrases to the user alongside with the search results. The user can then modify the original query using these phrases to narrow down the search. Query suggestion helps the users to easily navigate through the result set. For personal name queries, the key phrases extracted by our algorithm can be used as suggestions to reduce the ambiguity and narrow down the search on a particular namesake.

Social networking services (SNSs) have been given much attention on the Web recently. As a kind of online applications, SNSs can be used

*National Institute of Advanced Industrial Science and Technology

[1] www.google.com

Proceedings of the Workshop on How Can Computational Linguistics Improve Information Retrieval?, pages 17–24,
Sydney, July 2006.

to register and share personal information among friends and communities. There have been recent attempts to extract social networks using the information available on the Web [2](Mika, 2004; Matsuo et al., 2006). In both Matsuo's (2006) and Mika's (2004) algorithms, each person is represented by a node in the social network and the strength of the relationship between two people is represented by the length of the edge between the corresponding two nodes. As a measure of the strength of the relationship between two people *A* and *B*, these algorithms use the number of hits obtained for the query *A AND B*. However, this approach fails when *A* or *B* has namesakes because the number of hits in these cases includes the hits for the namesakes. To overcome this problem, we could include phrases in the query that uniquely identify *A* and *B* from their namesakes.

3 Related Work

Person name disambiguation can be seen as a special case of word sense disambiguation (WSD) (Schutze, 1998; McCarthy et al., 2004) problem which has been studied extensively in Natural Language Understanding. However, there are several fundamental differences between WSD and person name disambiguation. WSD typically concentrates on disambiguating between 2-4 possible meanings of the word, all of which are a priori known. However, in person name disambiguation in Web, the number of different namesakes can be much larger and unknown. From a resource point of view, WSD utilizes sense tagged dictionaries such as WordNet, whereas no dictionary can provide information regarding different namesakes for a particular name.

The problem of person name disambiguation has been addressed in the domain of research paper citations (Han et al., 2005), with various supervised methods proposed for its solution. However, citations have a fixed format compared to free text on the Web. Fields such as co-authors, title, journal name, conference name, year of publication can be easily extracted from a citation and provide vital information to the disambiguation process.

Research on multi-document person name resolution (Bagga and Baldwin, 1998; Mann and Yarowsky, 2003; Fleischman and Hovy, 2004) focuses on the related problem of determining if two instances with the same name and from different documents refer to the same individual. Bagga and Baldwin (1998) first perform within-document coreference resolution to form coreference chains for each entity in each document. They then use the text surrounding each reference chain to create summaries about each entity in each document. These summaries are then converted to a bag of words feature vector and are clustered using standard vector space model often employed in IR. The use of simplistic bag of words clustering is an inherently limiting aspect of their methodology. On the other hand, Mann and Yarowsky (2003) proposes a richer document representation involving automatically extracted features. However, their clustering technique can be basically used only for separating two people with the same name. Fleischman and Hovy (2004) constructs a maximum entropy classifier to learn distances between documents that are then clustered. Their method requires a large training set.

Pedersen et al. (2005) propose an unsupervised approach to resolve name ambiguity by representing the context of an ambiguous name using second order context vectors derived using singular value decomposition (SVD) on a co-occurrence matrix. They agglomeratively cluster the vectors using cosine similarity. They evaluate their method only on a conflated dataset of pseudonames, which begs the question of how well such a technique would fair on a more real-world challenge. Li et al. (2005) propose two approaches to disambiguate entities in a set of documents: a supervisedly trained pairwise classifier and an unsupervised generative model. However, they do not evaluate the effectiveness of their method in Web search.

Bekkerman and McCallum (2005) present two unsupervised methods for finding web pages referring to a particular person: one based on link structure and another using Agglomerative/Conglomerative Double Clustering (A/CDC). Their scenario focuses on simultaneously disambiguating an existing social network of people, who are closely related. Therefore, their method cannot be applied to disambiguate an individual whose social network (for example, friends, colleagues) is not known. Guha and Grag (2004) present a re-ranking algorithm to disambiguate people. The algorithm requires a user to select one of the returned pages as a starting point. Then,

[2]http://flink.sematicweb.org/. The system won the 1st place at the Semantic Web Challenge in ISWC2004.

Table 1: Data set for experiments

Collection	No of namesakes
person-X	4
Michael Jackson	3
Jim Clark	8
William Cohen	10

through comparing the person descriptions, the algorithm re-ranks the entire search results in such a way that pages referring to the same person described in the user-selected page are ranked higher. A user needs to browse the documents in order to find which matches the user's intended referent, which puts an extra burden on the user.

None of the above mentioned works attempt to extract key phrases to disambiguate person name queries, a contrasting feature in our work.

4 Data Set

We select three ambiguous names (*Micheal Jackson*, *William Cohen* and *Jim Clark*) that appear in previous work in name resolution. For each name we query *Google* with the name and download top 100 pages. We manually classify each page according to the namesakes discussed in the page. We ignore pages which we could not decide the namesake from the content. We also remove pages with images that do not contain any text. No pages were found where more than one namesakes of a name appear. For automated pseudo-name evaluation purposes, we select four names (*Bill Clinton*, *Bill Gates*, *Tom Cruise* and *Tiger Woods*) for conflation, who we presumed had one vastly predominant sense. We download 100 pages from Google for each person. We replace the name of the person by "person-X" in the collection, thereby introducing ambiguity. The structure of our dataset is shown in Table 1.

5 Method

5.1 Problem Statement

Given a collection of documents relevant to an ambiguous name, we assume that each document in the collection contains exactly one namesake of the ambiguous name. This is a fair assumption considering the fact that although namesakes share a common name, they specializes in different fields and have different Web appearances. Moreover, the one-to-one association between documents and people formed by this assumption, let us model the person name disambiguation problem as a one of hard-clustering of documents.

The outline of our method is as following; Given a set of documents representing a group of people with the same name, we represent each document in the collection using a *Term-Entity* model (section 5.2). We define a contextual similarity metric (section 5.4) and then cluster (section 5.5) the term-entity models using the contextual similarity between them. Each cluster is considered to be representing a different namesake. Finally, key phrases that uniquely identify each namesake are selected from the clusters. We perform experiments at each step of our method to evaluate its performance.

5.2 Term-Entity Model

The first step toward disambiguating a personal name is to identify the discriminating features of one person from another. In this paper we propose *Term-Entity models* to represent a person in a document.

Definition. *A term-entity model $T(A)$, representing a person A in a document D, is a boolean expression of n literals $a_1, a_2, \ldots, a_n$. Here, a boolean literal a_i is a multi-word term or a named entity extracted from the document D.*

For simplicity, we only consider boolean expressions that combine the literals through AND operator.

The reasons for using terms as well as named entities in our model are two fold. Firstly, there are multi-word phrases such as *secretary of state*, *racing car driver* which enable us to describe a person uniquely but not recognized by named entity taggers. Secondly, automatic term extraction (Frantzi and Ananiadou, 1999) can be done using statistical methods and does not require extensive linguistic resources such as named entity dictionaries, which may not be available for some domains.

5.3 Creating Term-Entity Models

We extract terms and named entities from each document to build the term-entity model for that document. For automatic multi-word term extraction, we use the *C-value* metric proposed by Frantzi et al. (1999). Firstly, the text from which we need to extract terms is tagged using a part of speech tagger. Then a linguistic filter and a stop words list constrain the word sequences that

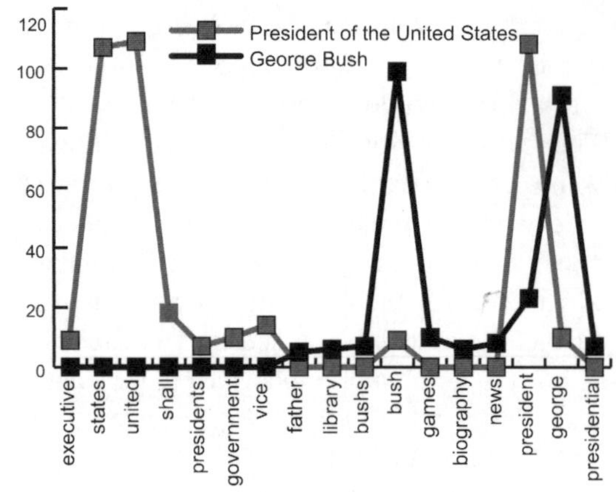

Figure 1: Distribution of words in snippets for "George Bush" and "President of the United States"

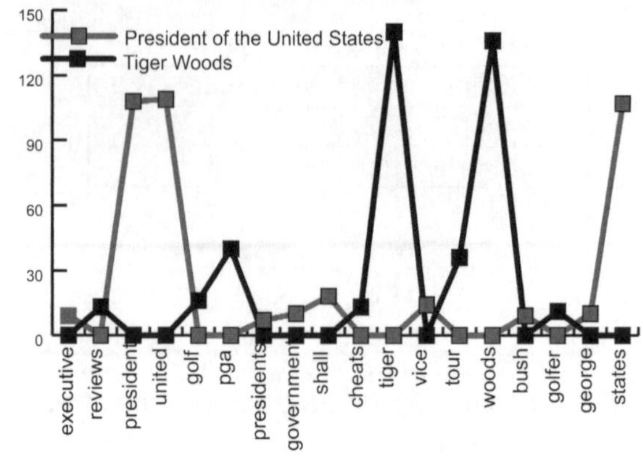

Figure 2: Distribution of words in snippets for "Tiger Woods" and "President of the United States"

are allowed as genuine multi-word terms. The linguistic filter contains a predefined set of patterns of nouns, adjectives and prepositions that are likely to be terms. The sequences of words that remain after this initial filtering process (candidate terms) are evaluated for their *termhood* (likeliness of a candidate to be a term) using C-value. C-value is built using statistical characteristics of the candidate string, such as, total frequency of occurrence of the candidate string in the document, the frequency of the candidate string as part of other longer candidate strings, the number of these longer candidate terms and the length of candidate string (in number of words). We select the candidates with higher C-values as terms (see (Frantzi and Ananiadou, 1999) for more details on C-value based term extraction).

To extract entities for the term-entity model, the documents were annotated by a named entity tagger [3]. We select personal names, organization names and location names to be included in the term-entity model.

5.4 Contextual Similarity

We need to calculate the similarity between term-entity models derived from different documents, in order to decide whether they belong to the same namesake or not. WordNet [4] based similarity metrics have been widely used to compute the semantic similarity between words in sense disambiguation tasks (Banerjee and Pedersen, 2002; McCarthy et al., 2004). However, most of the terms and entities in our term-entity models are proper names or multi-word expressions which are not listed in WordNet.

Sahami et al. (2005) proposed the use of snippets returned by a Web search engine to calculate the semantic similarity between words. A snippet is a brief text extracted from a document around the query term. Many search engines provide snippets alongside with the link to the original document. Since snippets capture the immediate surrounding of the query term in the document, we can consider a snippet as the context of a query term. Using snippets is also efficient because we do not need to download the source documents. To calculate the contextual similarity between two terms (or entities), we first collect snippets for each term (or entity) and pool the snippets into a combined "bag of words". Each collection of snippets is represented by a word vector, weighted by the normalized frequency (i.e., frequency of a word in the collection is divided by the total number of words in the collection). Then, the contextual similarity between two phrases is defined as the inner product of their snippet-word vectors.

Figures 1 and 2 show the distribution of most frequent words in snippets for the queries "George Bush", "Tiger Woods" and "President of the United States". In Figure 1 we observe the words "george" and "bush" appear in snippets for the query "President of the United States", whereas in Figure 2 none of the high frequent words appears in snippets for both queries. Contextual

[3] The named entity tagger was developed by the Cognitive Computation Group at UIUC. http://L2R.cs.uiuc.edu/ cogcomp/eoh/ne.html

[4] http://wordnet.princeton.edu/perl/webwn

similarity calculated as the inner product between word vectors is 0.2014 for "George Bush" and "President of the United States", whereas the same is 0.0691 for "Tiger Woods" and "President of the United States". We define the similarity $\mathrm{sim}(T(A), T(B))$, between two term-entity models $T(A) = \{a_1, \ldots, a_n\}$ and $T(B) = \{b_1, \ldots, b_m\}$ of documents A and B as follows,

$$\mathrm{sim}(T(A), T(B)) = \frac{1}{n} \sum_{i=1}^{n} \max_{1 \leq j \leq m} |a_i| \cdot |b_j|. \quad (1)$$

Here, $|a_i|$ represents the vector that contains the frequency of words that appear in the snippets for term/entity a_i. Contextual similarity between terms/entities a_i and b_j, is defined as the inner product $|a_i| \cdot |b_j|$. Without a loss of generality we assume $n \leq m$ in formula 1.

5.5 Clustering

We use Group-average agglomerative clustering (GAAC) (Cutting et al., 1992), a hybrid of single-link and complete-link clustering, to group the documents that belong to a particular namesake. Initially, we assign a separate cluster for each of the documents in the collection. Then, GAAC in each iteration executes the merger that gives rise to the cluster Γ with the largest average correlation $C(\Gamma)$ where,

$$C(\Gamma) = \frac{1}{2} \frac{1}{|\Gamma|(|\Gamma| - 1)} \sum_{u \in \Gamma} \sum_{v \in \Gamma} \mathrm{sim}(T(u), T(v)) \quad (2)$$

Here, $|\Gamma|$ denotes the number of documents in the merged cluster Γ; u and v are two documents in Γ and $\mathrm{sim}(T(u), T(v))$ is given by equation 1. Determining the total number of clusters is an important issue that directly affects the accuracy of disambiguation. We will discuss an automatic method to determine the number of clusters in section 6.3.

5.6 Key phrases Selection

GAAC process yields a set of clusters representing each of the different namesakes of the ambiguous name. To select key phrases that uniquely identify each namesake, we first pool all the terms and entities in all term-entity models in each cluster. For each cluster we select the most discriminative terms/entities as the key phrases that uniquely identify the namesake represented by that cluster from the other namesakes. We achieve this in two steps. In the first step, we reduce the number of terms/entities in each cluster by removing terms/entities that also appear in other clusters. In the second step, we select the terms/entities in each cluster according to their relevance to the ambiguous name. We compute the contextual similarity between the ambiguous name and each term/entity and select the top ranking terms/entities from each cluster.

6 Experiments and Results

6.1 Evaluating Contextual Similarity

In section 5.4, we defined the similarity between documents (i.e., term-entity models created from the documents) using a web snippets based contextual similarity (Formula 1). However, how well such a metric represents the similarity between documents, remains unknown. Therefore, to evaluate the contextual similarity among documents, we group the documents in "person-X" dataset into four classes (each class representing a different person) and use Formula 1 to compute within-class and cross-class similarity histograms, as illustrated in Figure 3.

Ideally, within-class similarity distribution should have a peak around 1 and cross-class similarity distribution around 0, whereas both histograms in Figure 3(a) and 3(b) have their peaks around 0.2. However, within-class similarity distribution is heavily biased toward to the right of this peak and cross-class similarity distribution to the left. Moreover, there are no document pairs with more than 0.5 cross-class similarity. The experimental results guarantees the validity of the contextual similarity metric.

6.2 Evaluation Metric

We evaluate experimental results based on the confusion matrix, where $A[i.j]$ represents the number of documents of "person i" predicted as "person j" in matrix A. $A[i, i]$ represents the number of correctly predicted documents for "person i". We define the disambiguation accuracy as the sum of diagonal elements divided by the sum of all elements in the matrix.

6.3 Cluster Quality

Each cluster formed by the GAAC process is supposed to be representing a different namesake. Ideally, the number of clusters formed should be equal to the number of different namesakes for

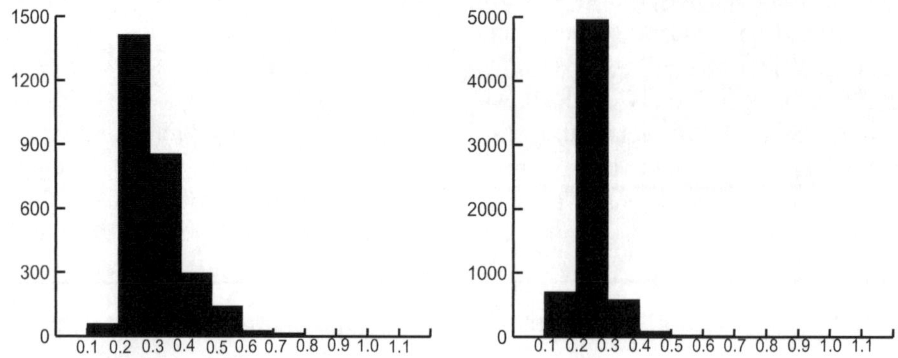

(a) Within-class similarity distribution in "person-X" dataset

(b) Cross-class similarity distribution in "person-X" dataset

Figure 3: The histogram of within-class and cross-class similarity distributions in "person-X" dataset. X axis represents the similarity value. Y axis represents the number of document pairs from the same class (within-class) or from different classes (cross-class) that have the corresponding similarity value.

the ambiguous name. However, in reality it is impossible to exactly know the number of namesakes that appear on the Web for a particular name. Moreover, the distribution of pages among namesakes is not even. For example, in the "Jim Clark" dataset 78% of documents belong to the two famous namesakes (*CEO Nestscape* and *Formula one world champion*). The rest of the documents are distributed among the other six namesakes. If these outliers get attached to the otherwise pure clusters, both disambiguation accuracy and key phrase selection deteriorate. Therefore, we monitor the *quality* of clustering and terminate further agglomeration when the cluster quality drops below a pre-set threshold. Numerous metrics have been proposed for evaluating quality of clustering (Kannan et al., 2000). We use normalized cuts (Shi and Malik, 2000) as a measure of cluster-quality.

Let, V denote the set of documents for a name. Consider, $A \subseteq V$ to be a cluster of documents taken from V. For two documents x,y in V, $\mathrm{sim}(x, y)$ represents the contextual similarity between the documents (Formula 1). Then, the normalized cut $N_{cut}(A)$ of cluster A is defined as,

$$N_{cut}(A) = \frac{\sum_{x \in A\, y \in (V-A)} \mathrm{sim}(x, y)}{\sum_{x \in A\, y \in V} \mathrm{sim}(x, y)}. \quad (3)$$

For a set, $\{A_1, \ldots, A_n\}$ of non-overlapping n clusters A_i, we define the *quality* of clustering,

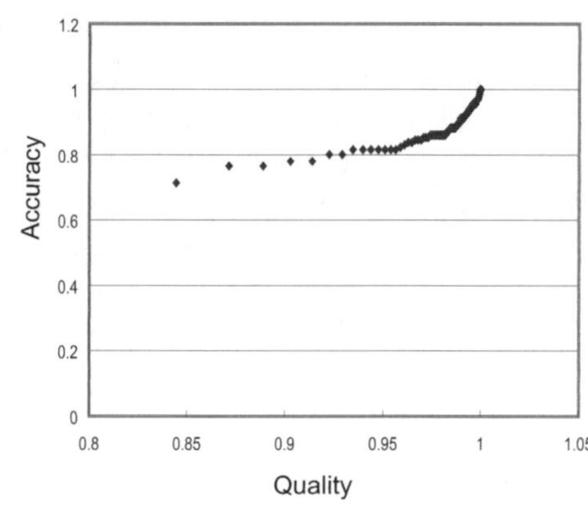

Figure 4: Accuracy Vs Cluster Quality for person-X data set.

$\mathrm{Quality}(\{A_1, \ldots, A_n\})$, as follows,

$$\mathrm{Quality}(\{A_1, \ldots, A_n\}) = \frac{1}{n} \sum_{i=1}^{n} N_{cut}(A_i). \quad (4)$$

To explore the faithfulness of cluster quality in approximating accuracy, we compare accuracy (calculated using human-annotated data) and cluster quality (automatically calculated using Formula 4) for person-X data set. Figure 4 shows cluster quality in x-axis and accuracy in y-axis. We observe a high correlation (Pearson coefficient of 0.865) between these two measures, which enables us to guide the clustering process through cluster quality.

When cluster quality drops below a pre-defined

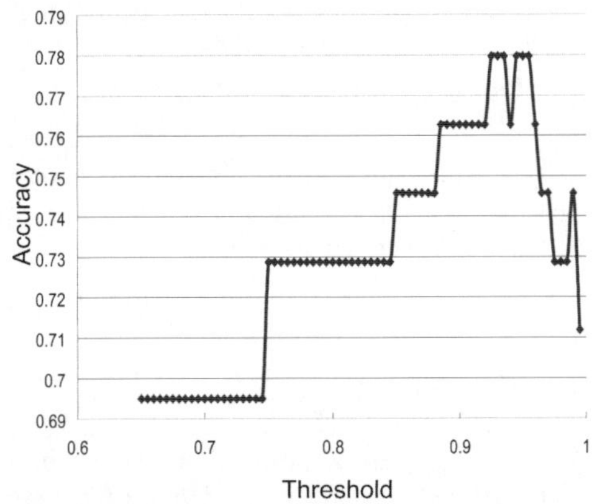

Figure 5: Accuracy Vs Threshold value for person-X data set.

threshold, we terminate further clustering. We assign the remaining documents to the already formed clusters based on the correlation (Formula 2) between the document and the cluster. To determine the threshold of cluster quality, we use person-X collection as training data. Figure 5 illustrates the variation of accuracy with threshold. We select threshold at 0.935 where accuracy maximizes in Figure 5. Threshold was fixed at 0.935 for the rest of the experiments.

6.4 Disambiguation Accuracy

Table 2 summarizes the experimental results. The baseline, majority sense , assigns all the documents in a collection to the person that have most documents in the collection. Proposed method outperforms the baseline in all data sets. Moreover, the accuracy values for the proposed method in Table 2 are statistically significant (t-test: P(T≤t)=0.0087, $\alpha = 0.05$) compared to the baseline. To identify each cluster with a namesake, we chose the person that has most number of documents in the cluster. "Found" column shows the number of correctly identified namesakes as a fraction of total namesakes. Although the proposed method correctly identifies the popular namesakes, it fails to identify the namesakes who have just one or two documents in the collection.

6.5 Web Search Task

Key phrases extracted by the proposed method are listed in Figure 6 (Due to space limitations, we show only the top ranking key phrases for two collections). To evaluate key phrases in disambiguating namesakes, we set up a web search experiment as follows. We search for the ambiguous name and the key phrase (for example, *"Jim Clark"* AND *"racing driver"*) and classify the top 100 results according to their relevance to each namesake. Results of our experiment on *Jim Clark* dataset for the top ranking key phrases are shown in Table 3.

Table 2: Disambiguation accuracy for each collection.

Collection	Majority Sense	Proposed Method	Found Correct
person-X	0.3676	0.7794	4/4
Michael Jackson	0.6470	0.9706	2/3
Jim Clark	0.4407	0.7627	3/8
William Cohen	0.7614	0.8068	3/10

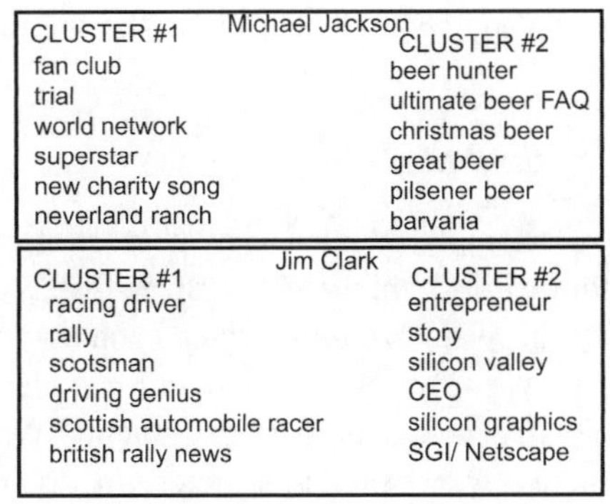

Figure 6: Top ranking key phrases in clusters for *Michael Jackson* and *Jim Clark* datasets.

In Table 3 we classified Google search results into three categories. "person-1" is the formula one racing world champion, "person -2" is the founder of Netscape and "other" category contains rest of the pages that we could not classify to previous two groups [5]. We first searched Google without adding any key phrases to the name. Including terms *racing diver*, *rally* and *scotsman*,

Table 3: Effectiveness of key phrases in disambiguating namesakes.

Phrase	person-1	person-2	others	Hits
NONE	41	26	33	1,080,000
racing driver	81	1	18	22,500
rally	42	0	58	82,200
scotsman	67	0	33	16,500
entrepreneur	1	74	25	28,000
story	17	53	30	186,000
silicon valley	0	81	19	46,800

[5] some of these pages were on other namesakes and some were not sufficiently detailed to properly classify

which were the top ranking terms for *Jim Clark* the formula one champion, yields no results for the other popular namesake. Likewise, the key words *entrepreneur* and *silicon valley* yield results fort he founder of Netscape. However, the key word *story* appears for both namesakes. A close investigation revealed that, the keyword *story* is extracted from the title of the book "The New New Thing: A Silicon Valley Story", a book on the founder of Netscape.

7 Conclusion

We proposed and evaluated a key phrase extraction algorithm to disambiguate people with the same name on the Web. We represented each document with a term-entity model and used a contextual similarity metric to cluster the documents. We also proposed a novel approach to determine the number of namesakes. Our experiments with pseudo and naturally ambiguous names show a statistically significant improvement over the baseline method. We evaluated the key phrases extracted by the algorithm in a web search task. The web search task reveals that including the key phrases in the query considerably reduces ambiguity. In future, we plan to extend the proposed method to disambiguate other types of entities such as location names, product names and organization names.

References

A. Bagga and B. Baldwin. 1998. Entity-based cross-document coreferencing using the vector space model. In *Proceedings of COLING*, pages 79–85.

Satanjeev Banerjee and Ted Pedersen. 2002. An adapted lesk algorithm for word sense disambiguation using word net. In *Proceedings of the third international conference on computational linguistics and intelligent text processing*, pages 136–145.

Ron Bekkerman and Andrew McCallum. 2005. Disambiguating web appearances of people in a social network. In *Proceedings of the 14th international conference on World Wide Web*, pages 463–470.

Douglass R. Cutting, Jan O. Pedersen, David Karger, and John W. Tukey. 1992. Scatter/gather: A cluster-based approach to browsing large document collections. In *Proceedings SIGIR '92*, pages 318–329.

M.B. Fleischman and E. Hovy. 2004. Multi-document person name resolution. In *Proceedings of 42nd Annual Meeting of the Association for Computational Linguistics (ACL), Reference Resolution Workshop*.

K.T. Frantzi and S. Ananiadou. 1999. The c-value/nc-value domain independent method for multi-word term extraction. *Journal of Natural Language Processing*, 6(3):145–179.

S. Gauch and J. B. Smith. 1991. Search improvement via automatic query reformulation. *ACM Trans. on Information Systems*, 9(3):249–280.

R. Guha and A. Garg. 2004. Disambiguating people in search. In *Stanford University*.

Hui Han, Hongyuan Zha, and C. Lee Giles. 2005. Name disambiguation in author citations using a k-way spectral clustering method. In *Proceedings of the International Conference on Digital Libraries*.

Ravi Kannan, Santosh Vempala, and Adrian Vetta. 2000. On clusterings: Good, bad, and spectral. In *Proceedings of the 41st Annual Symposium on the Foundation of Computer Science*, pages 367–380.

Xin Li, Paul Morie, and Dan Roth. 2005. Semantic integration in text, from ambiguous names to identifiable entities. *AI Magazine, American Association for Artificial Intelligence*, Spring:45–58.

Gideon S. Mann and David Yarowsky. 2003. Unsupervised personal name disambiguation. In *Proceedings of CoNLL-2003*, pages 33–40.

Y. Matsuo, J. Mori, and M. Hamasaki. 2006. Polyphonet: An advanced social network extraction system. In *to appear in World Wide Web Conference (WWW)*.

D. McCarthy, R. Koeling, J. Weeds, and J. Carroll. 2004. Finding predominant word senses in untagged text. In *Proceedings of the 42nd Meeting of the Association for Computational Linguistics (ACL'04)*, pages 279–286.

P. Mika. 2004. Bootstrapping the foaf-web: and experiment in social networking network minning. In *Proceedings of 1st Workshop on Friend of a Friend, Social Networking and the Semantic Web*.

Ted Pedersen, Amruta Purandare, and Anagha Kulkarni. 2005. Name discrimination by clustering similar contexts. In *Proceedings of the Sixth International Conference on Intelligent Text Processing and Computational Linguistics*.

Mehran Sahami and Tim Heilman. 2005. A web-based kernel function for matching short text snippets. In *International Workshop located at the 22nd International Conference on Machine Learning (ICML 2005)*.

Hinrich Schutze. 1998. Automatic word sense discrimination. *Computational Linguistics*, 24(1):97–123.

Jianbo Shi and Jitendra Malik. 2000. Normalized cuts and image segmentation. *IEEE Transactions on Pattern Analysis and Machine Intelligence*, 22(8):888–905.

How to Find Better Index Terms Through Citations

Anna Ritchie
University of Cambridge
Computer Laboratory
15 J J Thompson Avenue
Cambridge, CB3 0FD, U.K.
ar283@cl.cam.ac.uk

Simone Teufel
University of Cambridge
Computer Laboratory
15 J J Thompson Avenue
Cambridge, CB3 0FD, U.K.
sht25@cl.cam.ac.uk

Stephen Robertson
Microsoft Research Ltd
Roger Needham House
7 J J Thomson Avenue
Cambridge, CB3 0FB, U.K.
ser@microsoft.com

Abstract

We consider the question of how information from the textual context of citations in scientific papers could improve indexing of the cited papers. We first present examples which show that the context should in principle provide better and new index terms. We then discuss linguistic phenomena around citations and which type of processing would improve the automatic determination of the right context. We present a case study, studying the effect of combining the existing index terms of a paper with additional terms from papers citing that paper in our corpus. Finally, we discuss the need for experimentation for the practical validation of our claim.

1 Introduction

Information Retrieval (IR) is an established field and, today, the 'conventional' IR task is embodied by web searching. IR is mostly *term-based*, relying on the words within documents to describe them and, thence, try to determine which documents are relevant to a given user query. There are theoretically motivated and experimentally validated techniques that have become standard in the field. An example is the Okapi model; a probabilistic function for term weighting and document ranking (Spärck Jones, Walker & Robertson 2000). IR techniques using such statistical models almost always outperform more linguistically based ones. So, as statistical models are developed and refined, it begs the question 'Can Computational Linguistics improve Information Retrieval?'

Our particular research involves IR on scientific papers. There are definite parallels between the web and scientific literature, such as hyperlinks between webpages alongside citation links between papers. However, there are also fundamental differences, like the greater variability of webpages and the independent quality control of academic texts through the peer review process. The analogy between hyperlinks and citations itself is not perfect: whereas the number of hyperlinks varies greatly from webpage to webpage, the number of citations in papers is more constrained, due to the combination of strict page limits, the need to cite to show awareness of other work and the need to conserve space by including only the most relevant citations. Thus, while some aspects of web-based techniques will carry across to the current research domain, others will probably not. We are interested in investigating which lessons learned from web IR can successfully be applied to this slightly different domain.

2 Index Terms Through Link Structure

We aim to improve automatic indexing of scientific papers by finding additional index terms outside of the documents themselves. In particular, we believe that good index terms can be found by following the link structure between documents.

2.1 Hyperlinks

There is a wealth of literature on exploiting link structure between web documents for IR, including the 'sharing' of index terms between hyperlinked pages. Bharat & Mihaila (2001), for instance, propagate title and header terms to the pointed-to page, while Marchiori (1997) recursively augments the textual content of a page with *all* the text of the pages it points to.

Research has particularly concentrated on anchor text as a good place to find index terms, i.e.,

Proceedings of the Workshop on How Can Computational Linguistics Improve Information Retrieval?, pages 25–32,
Sydney, July 2006. ©2006 Association for Computational Linguistics

the text enclosed in the ⟨a⟩ tags of the HTML document. It is a well-documented problem that webpages are often poorly self-descriptive (e.g., Brin & Page 1998, Kleinberg 1999). For instance, www.google.com does not contain the phrase *search engine*. Anchor text, on the other hand, is often a higher-level description of the pointed-to page. Davison (2000) provides a good discussion of just how well anchor text does this and provides experimental results to back this claim. Thus, beginning with McBryan (1994), there is a trend of propagating anchor text along its hyperlink to associate it with the linked page, as well as that in which it is found. Google, for example, includes anchor text as index terms for the linked page (Brin & Page 1998).

Extending beyond anchor text, Chakrabarti et al. (1998) look for topic terms in a window of text around hyperlinks and weight that link accordingly, in the framework of a link structure algorithm, HITS (Kleinberg 1999).

2.2 Citations

The anchor text phenomenon is also observed with citations: they are introduced purposefully alongside some descriptive reference to the cited document. Thus, this text should contain good index terms for the cited document. In the following sections, we motivate the use of reference terms as index terms for cited documents, firstly, with some citation examples and, secondly, by discussing previous work.

Examples: Reference Terms as Index Terms

Figure 1 shows some citations that exemplify why reference terms should be good index terms for the cited document. (1) is an example of a citation with intuitively good index terms (those underlined) for the cited paper around it; a searcher looking for papers about a *learning system*, particularly one that uses *theory refinement* and/or one that learns *non-recursive NP and VP structures* might be interested in the paper, as might those searching for information about *ALLiS*.

The fact that an author has chosen those particular terms in referring to the paper means that they reflect what that author feels is important about the paper. It is reasonable, then, that other researchers interested in the same things would find the cited paper useful and could plausibly use such terms as query terms. It is true that the cited paper may well contain these terms, and they may even be important, prominent terms, but this is not necessarily the case. There are numerous situations in which the terms in the document are not the best indicators of what is important in it. Firstly, what is important in a paper in terms of what it is known and cited for is not always the same as what is important in it in terms of subject matter or focus. Secondly, what are considered to be the important contributions of a paper may change over time. Thirdly, the terminology used to describe the important contributions may be different from that used in the paper or may change over time.

(2) exemplifies this special case, where a paper is referred to using terms that are not in the paper itself: the cited paper is the standard reference for the HITS algorithm yet the name HITS was only attributed to the algorithm after the paper was written and it doesn't contain the term at all[1].

The last two examples show how citing authors can provide higher level descriptions of the cited paper, e.g., *good overview* and *comparison*. These meta-descriptors are less likely to appear in the papers themselves as prominent terms yet, again, could plausibly be used as query terms for a searcher.

Reference Directed Indexing

These examples (and many more) suggest that text used in reference to papers can provide useful index terms, just as anchor text does for webpages. Bradshaw & Hammond (2002) even go so far as to argue that reference is more valuable as a source of index terms than the document's own content. Bradshaw's theory is that, when citing, authors describe a document in terms similar to a searcher's query for the information it contains.

However, there *is* no anchor text, per se, in papers, i.e., there are no HTML tags to delimit the text associated with a citation, unlike in webpages. The question is raised, therefore, of what is the anchor text equivalent for formal citations. Bradshaw (2003) extracts NPs from a fixed window of around one hundred words around the citation and uses these as the basis of his *Reference-Directed Indexing* (RDI).

Bradshaw evaluates RDI by, first, indexing documents provided by Citeseer (Lawrence, Bollacker & Giles 1999). A set of 32 queries was created by randomly selecting keyword phrases from

[1] There is a poetic irony in this: Kleinberg's paper notes the analagous problem of poorly self-descriptive webpages.

(1) ALLiS (Architecture for Learning Linguistic Structures) is a learning system which uses theory refinement in order to learn non-recursive NP and VP structures (Dejean, 2000).

(2) Such estimation is simplified from HITS algorithm (Kleinberg, 1998).

(3) As two examples, (Rabiner, 1989) and (Charniak et al., 1993) give good overviews of the techniques and equations used for Markov models and part-of-speech tagging, but they are not very explicit in the details that are needed for their application.

(4) For a comparison to other taggers, the reader is referred to (Zavrel and Daelemans, 1999).

Figure 1: Citations Motivating Reference Index Terms

24 documents in the collection with an author-written keywords section. Document relevance was determined by judging whether it addressed the same topic as the topic in the query source paper that is identified by the query keywords. Thus, the performance of RDI was compared to that of a standard vector-space model implementation (TF*IDF term weighting and cosine similarity retrieval), with RDI achieving better precision at top 10 documents (0.484 compared to 0.318, statistically significant at 99.5% confidence).

Citing Statements

In a considerably earlier study, closer to our own project, O'Connor (1982) motivated the use of words from *citing statements* as additional terms to augment an existing document representation. Though O'Connor did not have machine-readable documents, procedures for 'automatic' recognition of citing statements were developed and manually carried out on a collection of chemistry journal articles.

Proceeding from the sentence in which a citation is found, a set of hand-crafted, mostly sentence-based rules were applied to select the parts of the citing paper that conveyed information about the cited paper. For instance, the citing sentence, S, was always selected. If S contained a *connector* (a keyword, e.g., this, similarly, former) in its first twelve words, its predecessor, S_{-1}, was also selected etc. The majority of rules selected sentences from the text; others selected titles and words from tables, figures and captions.

The selected statements (minus stop words) were added to an existing representation for the cited documents, comprising human index terms and title and abstract terms, and a small-scale retrieval experiment was performed. A 20% increase in recall was found using the citing statements in addition to the existing index terms, though in a follow-up study on biomedical papers, the increase was only 4%[2] (O'Connor 1983).

O'Connor concludes that citing statements can aid retrieval but notes the inherent difficulty in identifying them. Some of the selection rules were only semi-automatic (e.g., required human identification of an article as a review) and most relied on knowledge of sentence boundaries, which is a non-trivial problem in itself. In all sentence-based cases, sentences were either selected in their entirety or not at all and O'Connor notes this as a source of falsely assigned terms.

3 Complex Citation Contexts

There is evidence, therefore, that good index terms for scholarly documents can be found in the documents that cite them. Identifying which terms around a citation really refer to it, however, is non-trivial. In this section, we discuss some examples of citations where this is the case and propose potential ways in which computational linguistics techniques may be useful in more accurately locating those reference terms. We take as our theoretical baseline all terms in a fixed window around a citation.

3.1 Examples: Finding Reference Terms

The first two examples in Figure 2 illustrate how the amount of text that refers to a citation can vary. Sometimes, only two or three terms will refer to a citation, as is often the case in enumerations such as (5). On the other hand, (6) shows a citation where much of the following section refers to the cited work. When a paper is heavily based on previous work, for example, extensive text may be afforded to describing that work in detail. Thus, this context could contribute dozens of legitimate index terms. A fixed size window around a citation

[2]O'Connor attributes this to a lower average number of citing papers in the biomedical domain.

(5) *Similar advances have been made in machine translation (Frederking and Nirenburg, 1994), speech recognition (Fiscus, 1997) and named entity recognition (Borthwick et al., 1998).*

(6) *Brown et al. (1993) proposed a series of statistical models of the translation process. IBM translation models try to model the translation probability ... which describes the relationship between a source language sentence ... and a target language sentence ... . In statistical alignment models ... a 'hidden' alignment ... is introduced, which describes a mapping from a target position ... to a source position ... . The relationship between the translation model and the alignment model is given by: ...*

(7) *The results of disambiguation strategies reported for pseudo-words and the like are consistently above 95% overall accuracy, far higher than those reported for disambiguating three or more senses of polysemous words (Wilks et al. 1993; Leacock, Towell, and Voorhees 1993).*

(8) *This paper concentrates on the use of zero, pronominal, and nominal anaphora in Chinese generated text. We are not concerned with lexical anaphora (Tutin and Kittredge 1992) where the anaphor and its antecedent share meaning components, while the anaphor belongs to an open lexical class.*

(9) *Previous work on the generation of referring expressions focused on producing minimal distinguishing descriptions (Dale and Haddock 1991; Dale 1992; Reiter and Dale 1992) or descriptions customized for different levels of hearers (Reiter 1990). Since we are not concerned with the generation of descriptions for different levels of users, we look only at the former group of work, which aims at generating descriptions for a subsequent reference to distinguish it from the set of entities with which it might be confused.*

(10) *Ferro et al. (1999) and Buchholz et al. (1999) both describe learning systems to find GRs. The former (TR) uses transformation-based error-driven learning (Brill and Resnik, 1994) and the latter (MB) uses memory-based learning (Daelemans et al., 1999).*

Figure 2: Citations Motivating Computational Linguistics

would not capture all the terms referring to it and only those.

In list examples such as (5), where multiple citations are in close proximity, almost any window size would result in overlapping windows and in terms being attributed to the wrong citation(s), as well as the right one. In such examples, the presence of other citations indicates a change in reference term 'ownership'. The same is often true of sentence boundaries, as they often signal a change in topic. Citations frequently occur at the start of sentences, as in (6), where a different approach is introduced. Similarly, a citation at the end of a sentence, as in (7), often indicates the completion of the current topic. In both cases, the sentence boundary (c.f. topic change) is also the boundary of the reference text. The same arguments increasingly apply to paragraph and section boundaries.

(8) is another example where the reference text does not extend beyond the citation sentence, though the citation is not at a sentence boundary. Instead, the topic contrast is indicated by a linguictic cue, i.e., the negation in *We are not*. This illustrates another phenomenon of citations: in contrasting their work with others', researchers often explicitly state what their paper is *not* about. Intuitively, not only are these terms better descriptors of the cited rather than citing paper, they might even raise the question of whether one should go as far as *excluding* selected terms during indexing of the citing paper. We are not advocating this here, though, and note that, in practice, such terms would not have much impact on the document: we would expect them to have low term frequencies in comparison to the important terms in that document and in comparison to their frequencies in other documents where they *are* important.

(9) is another example of this negation effect (*We are not concerned with...*). Along with (10), it also shows how complex the mapping between reference terms and citations can be. Firstly, reference terms may belong to more than one cita-

tion. For instance, in (10), *describe learning systems to find GRs* refers to both *Ferro et al. (1999)* and *Buchholz et al. (1999)*. Here, the presence of a second citation does not end the domain of the first's reference text, indicated by the use of *both* and the conjunction between the citations. Similarly, *transformation-based error-driven learning* also refers to two citations but, in this case, they are on opposite sides of the reference text, i.e., *Ferro et al. (1999)* and *(Brill and Resnik, 1994)*. Moreover, there is an intervening citation that it does not refer to, i.e., *Buchholz et al. (1999)*. The same is true of *memory-based learning*.

4 Case Study

In this section, we study the effect of adding citation index terms to one document: *The Mathematics of Statistical Machine Translation: Parameter Estimation* from the Computational Linguistics journal[3]. Our experimental setting is a corpus of ~9000 papers in the ACL Anthology[4], a digital archive of computational linguistics research papers. We found 24 citations to the paper in 10 other Anthology papers (that we knew to have citations to this paper through an unrelated study). As a simulation of ideal processing, we then manually extracted the terms from those around those citations that specifically referred to the paper, henceforth *ideal reference terms*. Next, we extracted all terms from a fixed window of ~50 terms on either side (equivalent to Bradshaw (2003)'s window size), henceforth *fixed reference terms*. Finally, we calculated various term statistics, including IDF values across the corpus. All terms were decapitalized. We now attempt to draw a 'term profile' of the document, both before and after those reference terms are added to the document, and discuss the implications for IR.

4.1 Index Term Analysis

Table 1 gives the top twenty ideal reference terms ranked by their TF*IDF values in the original document. Note that we observe the effects on the relative rankings of the ideal reference terms only, since it is these hand-picked terms that we consider to be important descriptors for the document and whose statistics will be most affected by the inclusion of reference terms. To give an indication of their importance relative to other terms in the document, however, the second column in Table 1 gives the absolute rankings of these terms in the original document. These numbers confirm that our ideal reference terms are, in fact, relatively important in the document; indeed, the top five terms in the document are all ideal reference terms. Further down the ranking, the ideal reference terms become more 'diluted' with terms not picked from our 24 citations. An inspection revealed that many of these terms were French words from example translations, since the paper deals with machine translation between English and French. Thus, they were bad index terms, for our purposes.

Rank		TF*IDF	Term
Ideal	Doc		
1	1	351.73	french
2	2	246.52	alignments
3	3	238.39	fertility
4	4	212.20	alignment
5	5	203.28	cept
6	8	158.45	probabilities
7	9	150.74	translation
8	12	106.11	model
9	17	79.47	probability
10	18	78.37	models
11	19	78.02	english
12	21	76.23	parameters
13	24	71.77	connected
14	28	62.48	words
15	32	57.57	em
13	35	54.88	iterations
14	45	45.00	statistical
15	54	38.25	training
16	69	32.93	word
17	74	31.31	pairs
18	81	29.29	machine
19	83	28.53	empty
20	130	19.72	series

Table 1: Ideal Reference Term Ranking by TF*IDF

Hence, we observed the effect of adding, first, the ideal reference terms then, separately, the fixed reference terms to the document, summarized in Tables 2 to 5. Tables 2 and 3 show the terms with the largest differences in positions as a result of adding the ideal and fixed reference terms respectively.

For instance, *ibm*'s TF*IDF value more than doubled. The term *ibm* appears only six times in the document (and not even from the main text but from authors' institutions and one bibliography item) yet one of its major contributions is the machine translation models it introduced, now standardly referred to as 'the IBM models'. Con-

[3]http://www.aclweb.org/anthology/J93-2003.pdf

[4]http://www.aclweb.org/anthology/

Term	TF*IDF Δ	Doc+ideal	Ideal Rank Δ
ibm	24.24	37.46	28 → 20
generative	4.44	11.10	38 → 33
source	5.35	6.42	65 → 44
decoders	6.41	6.41	-- → 45
corruption	6.02	6.02	-- → 46
expectation	2.97	5.94	51 → 47
relationship	2.96	5.92	52 → 48
story	2.94	5.88	53 → 49
noisy-channel	5.75	5.75	-- →52
extract	1.51	7.54	41 → 38

Table 2: Term Ranking Changes (Ideal)

Term	TF*IDF Δ	Doc+fixed	Ideal Rank Δ
ibm	48.48	61.70	28 → 18
target	19.64	19.64	--→ 26
source	14.99	16.06	65 → 32
phrase-based	14.77	14.77	--→ 36
trained	14.64	19.52	43 → 27
approaches	11.03	11.03	-- → 41
parallel	9.72	17.81	34 → 29
generative	8.88	15.54	38 → 33
train	8.21	8.21	-- → 45
channel	6.94	6.94	-- → 55
expectation	5.93	8.90	51 → 44
learn	5.93	7.77	60 → 47

Table 3: Term Ranking Changes (Fixed)

Term	TF*IDF
decoders	6.41
corruption	6.02
noisy-channel	5.75
attainable	5.45
target	5.24
source-language	4.99
phrase-based	4.92
target-language	4.82
application-specific	4.40
train	4.10
intermediate	4.01
channel	3.47
approaches	3.01
combinations	1.70
style	2.12
add	1.32
major	1.16
due	0.83
considered	0.81
developed	0.78

Table 4: New Non-zero TF*IDF Terms (Ideal)

sequently, 'IBM' was contained in many citation contexts in citing papers, leading to an ideal reference term frequency of 11 for *ibm*. As a result, *ibm* is boosted eight places to rank 20. This exemplifies how reference terms can better describe a document, in terms of what searchers might plausibly look for (c.f. Example 2).

There were twenty terms that do not occur in the document itself but are nevertheless used by citing authors to describe it, shown in Tables 4 and 5. Many of these have high IDF values, indicating their distinctiveness in the corpus, e.g., *decoders* (6.41), *corruption* (6.02) and *noisy-channel* (5.75). This, combined with the fact that citing authors use these terms in describing the paper, means that these terms are intuitively high quality descriptors of the paper. Without the reference index terms, however, the paper would score zero for these terms as query terms.

Many more fixed reference terms were found per citation than ideal ones. This can introduce noise. In general, the TF*IDF values of ideal reference terms can only be further boosted by including more terms and a comparison of Tables 2 with 3 (or 4 with 5) shows that this is sometimes the case, e.g, *ibm* occurred a further eleven times in the fixed reference terms, doubling its increase in TF*IDF. However, instances of those terms that only occurred in the fixed reference terms did not, in fact, refer to the citation of the paper, by definition of the ideal reference terms. For instance, one such extra occurrence of *ibm* is from a sentence following the citation that describes the exact model used in the current work:

(11) *According to the IBM models (Brown et al., 1993), the statistical word alignment model can be generally represented as in Equation (1) ... In this paper, we use a simplified IBM model 4 (Al-Onaizan et al., 1999), which ...*

Here, the second occurrence refers to *(Al-Onaizan et al., 1999)* but, by its proximity to the citation to our example paper *(Brown et al., 1993)*, is picked up by the fixed window. Since the term was arguably not directly intended to describe our paper, then, a different term might equally have been used; one that was inappropriate as an index term. Table 6 lists the fixed reference terms that were not also in the ideal reference terms; almost 400 in total. The vast majority of these occur very infrequently which suggests that they should not greatly affect the term profile of the document. However, the argument for adding *good*, high IDF reference terms that are not in the document itself

Term	TF*IDF
target	19.64
phrase-based	14.77
approaches	11.03
train	8.21
channel	6.94
decoders	6.41
corruption	6.02
noisy-channel	5.75
attainable	5.45
source-language	4.99
target-language	4.82
application-specific	4.40
intermediate	4.01
combinations	3.40
style	2.12
considered	1.62
major	1.16
due	0.83
developed	0.78

Table 5: New Non-zero TF*IDF Terms (Fixed)

conversely applies to adding *bad* ones: an 'incorrect' reference term added to the document will have its TF*IDF pushed off the zero mark, giving it the potential to score against inappropriate query terms. If such a term is distinctive (i.e., has a high IDF), the effect may be significant. The term *giza*, for example, has an IDF of 6.34 and is the name of a particular tool that is not mentioned in our example paper. However, since the tool is used to train IBM models, the two papers in the example above are often cited by the same papers and in close proximity. This increases the chances of such terms being picked up as reference terms for the wrong citation by a fixed window, heightening the adverse effect on its term profile.

5 Discussion and Conclusions

It is not too hard to find examples of citations that show a fixed window size is suboptimal for finding terms used in reference to cited papers. In extracting the ideal reference terms from only 24 citations for our case study, we saw just how difficult it is to decide which terms refer to which citations. We, the authors, came across examples where it was ambiguous how many citations certain terms referred to, ones where knowledge of the cited papers was required to interpret the scope of the citation and ones where we simply did not agree. This is a highly complex indexing task; one which humans have difficulty with, one for which we expect low human agreement and, therefore, the type that computational linguistics struggles to achieve high performance on. We agree with O'Connor (1982) that it is hard. We make no claims that computational linguistics will provide a full solution.

Nevertheless, our examples suggest that even simple computational linguistics techniques should help to more accurately locate reference terms. While it may be impossible to automatically pick out each specific piece of text that does refer to a given citation, there is much scope for improvement over a fixed window. The examples in Section 2 suggest that altering the size of the window that is applied would be a good first step. Some form of text segmentation, whether it be full-blown discourse analysis or simple sentence boundary detection, may be useful in determining where the extent of the reference text is.

While the case study presented here highlights several interesting effects of using terms from around citations as additional index terms for the cited paper, it cannot answer questions about how successful a practical method based on these observations would be, over a using simple fixed window, for example. In order for any real improvement in IR, the term profile of a document would have to be significantly altered by the reference terms. Enough terms, in particular repeated terms, would have to be successfully found via citations for such a quantitative improvement. It is not clear that computational linguistic techniques will improve over the statistical effects of redundant data.

We are thus in the last stages of setting up a larger experiment that will shed more light on this question. The experimental setup requires data where there are a significant number of citations to a number of test documents and a significant number of reference set terms. We have recently presented a test collection of scientific research papers (Ritchie, Teufel & Robertson 2006), which we intend to use for this experiment.

References

Bharat, K. & Mihaila, G. A. (2001), When experts agree: using non-affiliated experts to rank popular topics, *in* 'Tenth International World Wide Web Conference', pp. 597–602.

Bradshaw, S. (2003), Reference directed indexing: Redeeming relevance for subject search in citation indexes., *in* 'ECDL', pp. 499–510.

Bradshaw, S. & Hammond, K. (2002), Automatically indexing documents: Content vs. reference, *in* 'Intelligent User Interfaces'.

TF	# Terms	Terms
13	1	asr
8	4	caption, closed, section, methods
7	2	method, sentences
6	4	describes, example, languages, system
5	6	corpus, dictionary, heuristic, large, paper, results
4	17	account, aligned, confidence, dependency, details, during, equation, generally, given, manual, measures, order, probabilistic, proposed, shown, simplified, systems, word-aligned
3	29	according, algorithm, applications, build, case, choosing, chunk, current, described, employed, equivalence, experiments, introduced, introduction, length, links, number, obtain, obtained, performance, performing, problem, produced, related, show, sum, true, types, work
2	64	adaptation, akin, approximate, bitext, calculated, called, categories, certain, chunks, common, consider, consists, domain-specific, error, estimation, experimental, extracted, families, feature, features, found, functions, generated, generic, giza, good, high, improve, information, input, iraq, knowledge, large-scale, lexicon, linked, log-linear, maximum, measure, notion, omitted, original, output, parameter, pick, position, practice, presents, quality, rate, represented, researchers, rock, role, sinhalese, takes, tamil, text-to-text, toolkit, transcripts, transcriptions, translations, version, word-based, word-to-word
1	252	access, accuracy, achieve, achieving, actual, addition, address, adopted, advance, advantages, aligning, amalgam, annotated, applied, apply, applying, approximated, association, asymmetric, augmented, availability, available, average, back-off, base, baum-welch, begin, bitexts, bunetsu, candidate, candidates, cat, central, chinese, choose, chunk-based, class, closely, collecting, combination, compare, compared, compares, computed, concludes, consequently, contributed, convention, corpora, correspondence, corrupts, cost, counts, coverage, crucial, currently, decades, decoding, defines, denote, dependent, depending, determine, dictionaries, direct, directions, disadvantages, distinction, dominated, dynamic, efforts, english-chinese, english-spanish, enumerate, eojeol, eq, equations, errors, evaluation, excellent, expansion, explicitly, extracts, failed, fairly, final, finally, fit, flat-start, followed, form, formalisms, formulation, generation, gis, give, grouped, hallucination, halogen, handle, heuristic-based, hidden, highly, hill-climbing, hmm-based, hypothesis, ideal, identified, identify, identity, immediate, implemented, improved, improves, incorporate, increase, influence, initial, initialize, inspired, interchanging, introduces, investigations, involve, kate, kind, learning, learns, letter, letters, lexical, likelihood, link, list, longer, lowercase, main, make, makes, mapping, maximal, maximizes, means, modeling, modified, names, needed, nitrogen, nodes, occupy, omitting, optimal, outperform, overcome, parse, parser, part, part-of-speech, path, performed, play, plays, popular, pos, positions, power, precision, probable, produce, programming, promising, real-valued, reason, recall, recent, recently, recognition, recursion, recursively, reduction, reductions, refine, relative, relying, renormalization, representation, require, requires, research, restricting, reveal, sample, sampling, satisfactory, segments, semantic, sequences, setting, shortcomings, showed, significant, significantly, similarity, similarly, simple, simplicity, situation, space, speech, spelling, state-of-the-art, step, strategies, string, strong, studies, summaries, summarization, supervised, syntactic, tags, task-specific, technique, techniques, technologies, terms, testing, threshold, translation-related, transliteration, tree, trees, trellis, type, underlying, unrealistic, unsupervised, uppercase, value, viterbi, wanted, ways, well-formedness, well-founded, widely, widespread, works, written, wtop, yasmet, years, yields

Table 6: Term Frequencies of 'Noisy' Reference Index Terms

Brin, S. & Page, L. (1998), 'The anatomy of a large-scale hypertextual Web search engine', *Computer Networks and ISDN Systems* **30**(1–7), 107–117.

Chakrabarti, S., Dom, B., Gibson, D., Kleinberg, J., Raghavan, P. & Rajagopalan, S. (1998), Automatic resource list compilation by analyzing hyperlink structure and associated text, *in* 'Seventh International World Wide Web Conference'.

Davison, B. D. (2000), Topical locality in the web, *in* 'Research and Development in Information Retrieval (SIGIR)', pp. 272–279.

Kleinberg, J. M. (1999), 'Authoritative sources in a hyperlinked environment', *Journal of the ACM* **46**(5), 604–632.

Lawrence, S., Bollacker, K. & Giles, C. L. (1999), Indexing and retrieval of scientific literature, *in* 'Conference on Information and Knowledge Management (CIKM)', pp. 139–146.

Marchiori, M. (1997), 'The quest for correct information on the Web: Hyper search engines', *Computer Networks and ISDN Systems* **29**(8–13), 1225–1236.

McBryan, O. (1994), GENVL and WWWW: Tools for taming the web, *in* 'First International World Wide Web Conference'.

O'Connor, J. (1982), 'Citing statements: Computer recognition and use to improve retrieval', *Information Processing and Management* **18**(3), 125–131.

O'Connor, J. (1983), 'Biomedical citing statements: Computer recognition and use to aid full-text retrieval', *Information Processing and Management* **19**, 361–368.

Ritchie, A., Teufel, S. & Robertson, S. (2006), Creating a test collection for citation-based IR experiments, *in* 'HLT-NAACL'.

Spärck Jones, K., Walker, S. & Robertson, S. E. (2000), 'A probabilistic model of information retrieval: development and comparative experiments - parts 1 & 2.', *Information Processing and Management* **36**(6), 779–840.

Exploring Semantic Constraints for Document Retrieval

Hua Cheng, Yan Qu, Jesse Montgomery, David A. Evans
Clairvoyance Corporation
5001 Baum Blvd., Suite 700, Pittsburgh, PA 15213, U.S.A.
{H.Cheng, Y.Qu, J.Montgomery, dae}@clairvoyancecorp.com

Abstract

In this paper, we explore the use of structured content as semantic constraints for enhancing the performance of traditional term-based document retrieval in special domains. First, we describe a method for automatic extraction of semantic content in the form of attribute-value (AV) pairs from natural language texts based on domain models constructed from a semi-structured web resource. Then, we explore the effect of combining a state-of-the-art term-based IR system and a simple constraint-based search system that uses the extracted AV pairs. Our evaluation results have shown that such combination produces some improvement in IR performance over the term-based IR system on our test collection.

1 Introduction

The questions of where and how sophisticated natural language processing techniques can improve traditional term-based information retrieval have been explored for more than a decade. A considerable amount of work has been carried out that seeks to leverage semantic information for improving traditional IR. Early TREC systems such as INQUERY handled both natural language and semi-structured queries and tried to search for constraint expressions for country and time etc. in queries (Croft et al., 1994). Later work, as discussed in (Strzalkowski et al., 1996), has focused on exploiting semantic information at the word level, including various attempts at word-sense disambiguation, e.g., (Voorhees, 1998), or the use of special-purpose terms; other approaches have looked at phrase-level indexing or full-text query expansion. No approaches to date, however, have sought to employ semantic information beyond the word level, such as that expressed by attribute-value (AV) pairs, to improve term-based IR.

Attribute-value pairs offer an abstraction for instances of many application domains. For example, a person can be represented by a set of attributes such as name, date-of-birth, job title, and home address, and their associated values; a house has a different set of attributes such as address, size, age and material; many product specifications can be mapped directly to AV pairs. AV pairs represent domain specific semantic information for domain instances.

Using AV pairs as semantic constraints for retrieval is related to some recent developments in areas such as Semantic Web retrieval, XML document retrieval, and the integration of IR and databases. In these areas, structured information is generally assumed. However, there is abundant and rich information that exists in unstructured text only. The goal of this work includes first to explore a method for automatically extracting structured information in the form of AV pairs from text, and then to utilize the AV pairs as semantic constraints for enhancing traditional term-based IR systems.

The paper is organized as follows. Section 2 describes our method of adding AV annotations to text documents that utilizes a domain model automatically extracted from the Web. Section 3 presents two IR systems using a vector space model and semantic constraints respectively, as well as a system that combines the two. Section 4 describes the data set and topic set for evaluating the IR systems. In Section 5, we compare the performance of the three IR systems, and draw initial conclusions on how NLP techniques can improve traditional IR in specific domains.

2 Domain-Driven AV Extraction

This section describes a method that automatically discovers attribute-value structures from unstructured texts, the result of which is represented as texts annotated with semantic tags.

Proceedings of the Workshop on How Can Computational Linguistics Improve Information Retrieval?, pages 33–40,
Sydney, July 2006.

We chose the digital camera domain to illustrate and evaluate the methodology described in this paper. We expect this method to be applicable to all domains whose main features can be represented as a set of specifications.

2.1 Construction of Domain Model

A domain model (DM) specifies a terminology of concepts, attributes and values for describing objects in a domain. The relationships between the concepts in such a model can be heterogeneous (e.g., the link between two concepts can mean inheritance or containment). In this work, a domain model is used for establishing a vocabulary as well as for establishing the attribute-value relationship between phrases.

For the digital camera domain, we automatically constructed a domain model from existing Web resources. Web sites such as epinions.com and dpreview.com generally present information about cameras in HTML tables generated from internal databases. By querying these databases and extracting table content from the dynamic web pages, we can automatically reconstruct the databases as domain models that could be used for NLP purposes. These models can optionally be organized hierarchically. Although domain models generated from different websites of the same domain are not exactly the same, they often share many common features.

From the epinions.com product specifications for 1157 cameras, we extracted a nearly comprehensive domain model for digital cameras, consisting of a set of attributes (or features) and their possible values. A portion of the model is represented as follows:

```
{Digital Camera}
    <Brand> <Price> <Lens>
{Brand}
    (57) Canon
    (33) Nikon
{Price} $
    (136) 100 - 200
    (100) >= 400
{Lens}
    <Optical Zoom> <Focus Range>
{Optical Zoom} x
    (17) 4
    (3) 2.5
{Focus Range} in., "
    (2) 3.9 - infinity
    (1) 12 - infinity
```

In this example, attributes are shown in curly brackets and sub-attributes in angle brackets. Attributes are followed by possible units for their numerical values. Values come below the attributes, headed by their frequencies in all specifications. The frequency information (in parentheses) is used to calculate term weights of attributes and values.

Specifications in HTML tables generally do not specify explicitly the type restrictions on values (even though the types are typically defined in the underlying databases). As type restrictions contain important domain information that is useful for value extraction, we recover the type restrictions by identifying patterns in values. For example, attributes such as *price* or *dimension* usually have numerical values, which can be either a single number ("$300"), a range ("$100 - $200"), or a multi-dimensional value ("4 in. x 3 in. x 2 in."), often accompanied by a unit, e.g., *$* or *inches*, whereas attributes such as *brand* and *accessory* usually have string values, e.g., "Canon" or "battery charger".

We manually compile a list of units for identifying numerical values, which is partially domain general. We identify range and multi-dimensional values using such patterns as "A – B", "A to B", "less than A", and "A x B", etc. Numerical values are then normalized to a uniform format.

2.2 Identification of AV Pairs

Based on the constructed domain model, we can identify domain values in unstructured texts and assign attribute names and domains to them. We focus on extracting values of a domain attribute. Attribute names appearing by themselves are not of interest here because attribute names alone cannot establish attribute-value relations. However, identification of attribute names is necessary for disambiguation.

The AV extraction procedure contains the following steps:

1. Use MINIPAR (Lin, 1998) to generate dependency parses of texts.
2. For all noun phrase chunks in parses, iteratively match sub-phrases of each chunk with the domain model to find all possible matches of attribute names and values above a threshold:
    - A chunk contains all words up to the noun head (inclusive);
    - Post-head NP components (e.g., PP and clauses) are treated as separate chunks.
3. Disambiguate values with multiple attribute assignments using the sentence context, with a preference toward closer context based on dependency.

4. Mark up the documents with XML tags that represent AV pairs.

Steps 2 and 3 are the center of the AV extraction process, where different strategies are employed to handle values of different types and where ambiguous values are disambiguated. We describe these strategies in detail below.

Numerical Value

Numerical values are identified based on the unit list and the range and multi-dimensional number patterns described earlier in Section 2.1. The predefined mappings between units and attributes suggest attribute assignment. It is possible that one unit can be mapped to multiple attributes. For example, "x" can be mapped to either optical zoom or digital zoom, both of which are kept as possible candidates for future disambiguation. For range and multi-dimensional numbers, we find all attributes in the domain model that have at least one matched range or multi-dimensional value, and keep attributes identified by either a unit or a pattern as candidates. Numbers without a unit can only be matched exactly against an existing value in the domain model.

String Value

Human users often refer to a domain entity in different ways in text. For example, a camera called "Canon PowerShot G2 Black Digital Camera" in our domain model is seldom mentioned exactly this way in ads or reviews, but rather as "Canon PowerShot G2", "Canon G2", etc. However, a domain model generally only records full name forms rather than their all possible variations. This makes the identification of domain values difficult and invalidates the use of a trained classifier that needs training samples consisting of a large variety of name references.

An added difficulty is that web texts often contain grammatical errors and incomplete sentences as well as large numbers of out-of-vocabulary words and, therefore, make the dependency parses very noisy. As a result, effectiveness of extraction algorithms based on certain dependency patterns can be adversely affected.

Our approach makes use of the more accurate parser functionalities of part-of-speech tagging and phrase boundary detection, while reducing the reliance on low level dependency structures. For noun phrase chunks extracted from parse trees, we iteratively match all sub-phrases of each chunk with the domain model to find matching attributes and values above a threshold. It is often possible to find multiple AV pairs in a single NP chunk.

Assigning domain attributes to an NP is essentially a classification problem. In our domain model, each attribute can be seen as a target class and its values as the training set. For a new phrase, the idea is to find the value in the domain model that is most similar and then assign the attribute of this nearest neighbor to the phrase. This motivates us to adopt K Nearest Neighbor (KNN) (Fix and Hodges, 1951) classification for handling NP values. The core of KNN is a similarity metric. In our case, we use word editing distance (Wagner and Fischer, 1974) that takes into account the cost of word insertions, deletions, and substitutions. We compute word editing distance using dynamic programming techniques.

Intuitively, words do not carry equal weights in a domain. In the earlier example, words such as "PowerShot" and "G2" are more important than "digital" and "camera", so editing costs for such words should be higher. This draws an analogy to the metric of Inverse Document Frequency (IDF) in the IR community, used to measure the discriminative capability of a term in a document collection. If we regard each value string as a document, we can use IDF to measure the weight of each term in a value string to emphasize important domain terms and de-emphasize more general ones. The normalized cost is computed as:

$$\log(TN/N)/\log(TN)$$

where TN is the total number of values for an attribute, and N is the number of values where a term occurs. This equation assigns higher cost to more discriminative terms and lower cost to more general terms. It is also used to compute costs of terms in attribute names. For words not appearing in a class the cost is 1, the maximum cost.

The distance between a new phrase and a DM phrase is then calculated using word editing cost based on the costs of substitution, insertion, and deletion, where

$$Cost_{sub} = (Cost_{DM} + Cost_{new}) / 2$$
$$Cost_{ins} = Cost_{new}$$
$$Cost_{del} = Cost_{DM}$$
$$Cost_{edit} = \min(Cost_{sub}, Cost_{ins}, Cost_{del})$$

where $Cost_{DM}$ is the cost of a word in a domain value (i.e., its normalized IDF score), and $Cost_{new}$

is that of a word in the new phrase. The cost is also normalized by the larger of the weighted lengths of the two phrases. We use a threshold of 0.6 to cut off phrases with higher cost.

For a phrase that returns only a couple of matches, the similarity, i.e., the matching probability, is computed as 1 - $Cost_{edit}$; otherwise, the similarity is the maximum likelihood of an attribute based on the number of returned values belonging to this attribute.

Disambiguation by Sentence Context

The AV identification process often returns multiple attribute candidates for a phrase that needs to be further disambiguated. The words close to the phrase usually provide good indications of the correct attribute names. Motivated by this observation, we design the disambiguation procedure as follows. First we examine the sibling nodes of the target phrase node in the dependency structure for a mention of an attribute name that overlaps with a candidate. Next, we recursively traverse upwards along the dependency tree until we find an overlap or reach the top of the tree. If an overlap is found, that attribute becomes the final assignment; otherwise, the attribute with the highest probability is assigned. This method gives priority to the context closest (in terms of dependency) to the target phrase. For example, in the sentence "The 4x stepless digital zoom lets you capture intricate details" (parse tree shown below), "4x" can be mapped to both optical zoom and digital zoom, but the sentence context points to the second candidate.

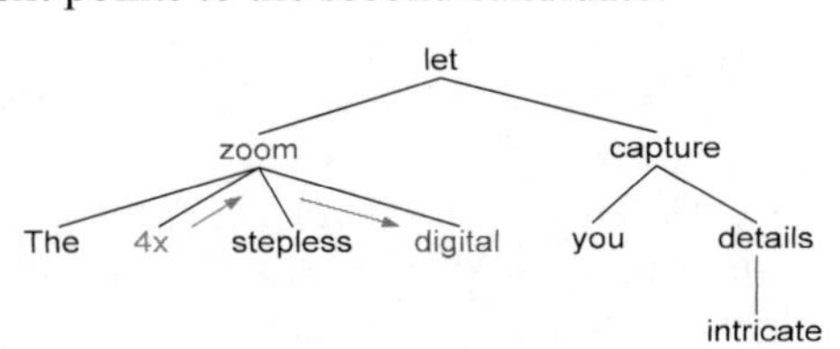

3 Document Retrieval Systems

This section introduces three document retrieval systems: the first one retrieves unstructured texts based on vector space models, the second one takes advantage of semantic structures constructed by the methods in Section 2, and the last one combines the first two systems.

3.1 Term-Based Retrieval (S1)

Our system for term-based retrieval from unstructured text is based on the CLARIT system, implementing a vector space retrieval model (Evans and Lefferts, 1995; Qu et al., 2005). The CLARIT system identifies terms in documents and constructs its index based on NLP-determined linguistic constituents (NPs, subphrases and words). The index is built upon full documents or variable-length subdocuments. We used subdocuments in the range of 8 to 12 sentences as the basis for indexing and scoring documents in our experiments.

Various similarity measures are supported in the model. For the experiments described in the paper, we used the dot product function for computing similarities between a query and a document:

$$sim(Q, D) = \sum_{t \in Q \cap D} W_Q(t) \cdot W_D(t).$$

where $W_Q(t)$ is the weight associated with the query term t and $W_D(t)$ is the weight associated with the term t in the document D. The two weights were computed as follows:

$$W_D(t) = TF_D(t) \cdot IDF(t).$$
$$W_Q(t) = C(t) \cdot TF_Q(t) \cdot IDF(t)$$

where IDF and TF are standard inverse document frequency and term frequency statistics, respectively. *IDF(t)* was computed with the target corpus for retrieval. The coefficient *C(t)* is an "importance coefficient", which can be modified either manually by the user or automatically by the system (e.g., updated during feedback).

For term-based document retrieval, we have also experimented with pseudo relevance feedback (PRF) with various numbers of retrieved documents and various numbers of terms from such documents for query expansion. While PRF did result in improvement in performance, it was not significant. This is probably due to the fact that in this restricted domain, there is not much vocabulary variation and thus the advantage of using query expansion is not fully realized.

3.2 Constraint-Based Retrieval (S2)

The constraint-based retrieval approach searches through the AV-annotated document collection based on the constraints extracted from queries. Given a query q, our constraint-based system scores each document in the collection by comparing the extracted AV pairs with the constraints in q. Suppose q has a constraint $c(a, v)$ that restricts the value of the attribute a to v, where v can be either a concrete value (e.g., 5 megapixels) or a range (e.g., less than $400). If a

is present in a document *d* with a value *v'* that satisfies *v*, that is, *v'* = *v* if *v* is a concrete value or *v'* falls in the range defined by *v*, *d* is given a positive score *w*. However, if *v'* does not satisfy *v*, then *d* is given a negative score *-w*. No mention of *a* does not change the score of *d*, except that, when *c* is a string constraint, we use a back-off model that awards *d* a positive score *w* if it contains *v* as a substring. The final score of *d* given *q* is the sum of all scores for each constraint in *q*, normalized by the maximum score for *q*: $\sum_{i=1}^{n} c_i w_i$, where c_i is one of the *n* constraints specified in *q* and w_i its score.

We rank the documents by their scores. This scoring schema facilitates a sensible cutoff point, so that a constraint-based retrieval system can return 0 or fewer than top N documents when a query has no or very few relevant documents.

3.3 Combined Retrieval (S3)

Lee (1997) analyzed multiple post-search data fusion methods using TREC3 ad hoc retrieval data and explained the combination of different search results on the grounds that different runs retrieve similar sets of relevant documents, but different sets of non-relevant documents. The combination methods therefore boost the ranks of the relevant documents. One method studied was the summation of individual similarities, which bears no significant difference from the best approach (i.e., further multiply the summation with the number of nonzero similarities).

Our system therefore adopts the summation method for its simplicity. Because the scores from term-based and constraint-based retrieval are normalized, we simply add them together for each document retrieved by both approaches and re-rank the documents based on their new scores. More sophisticated combination methods can be explored here, such as deciding which score to emphasize based on the characterizations of the queries, e.g., whether a query has more numerical values or string values.

4 Experimental Study

In this section, we describe the experiments we performed to investigate combining terms and semantic constraints for document retrieval.

4.1 Data Sets

To construct a domain corpus, we used search results from craigslist.org. We chose the "for sale – electronics" section for the "San Francisco Bay Area". We then submitted the search term "digital camera" in order to retrieve advertisements. After manually removing duplicates and expired ads, our corpus consisted of 437 ads posted between 2005-10-28 and 2005-11-07. A typical ad is illustrated below, with a small set of XML tags specifying the fields of the title of the ad (*title*), date of posting (*date*), ad body (*text*), ad id (*docno*), and document (*doc*). The length of the documents varies considerably, from 5 or 6 sentences to over 70 (with specifications copied from other websites). The ads have an average length of 230 words.

```
<doc>
  <docno>docid519</docno>
  <title>brand new 12 mega pixel digital camera</title>
  <date>2005-11-07, 8:27AM PST</date>
  <text>
    BRAND NEW 12 mega pixel digital camera.............only $400,
      -12 Mega pixels (4000x3000) Max Resolution
      -2.0 Color LCD Display
      -8x Digital Zoom
      -16MB Built-In (internal) Memory
      -SD or MMC card (external) Memory
      -jpeg picture format
    ALSO COMES WITH SOFTWARE & CABLES
  </text>
</doc>
```

The test queries were constructed based on human written questions from the Digital Photography Review website (www.dpreview.com) Q&A forums, which contain discussions from real users about all aspects of digital photography. Often, users ask for suggestions on purchasing digital cameras and formulate their needs as a set of constraints. These queries form the base of our topic collection.

The following is an example of such a topic manually annotated with the semantic constraints of interest to the user:

```
<topic>
  <id>1</id>
  <query>
    I wanted to know what kind of Digital SLR camera I should buy. I plan to spend nothing higher than $1500. I was told to check out the Nikon D70.
  </query>
  <constraint>
    <hard: type = "SLR" />
    <hard: price le $1500 />
    <soft: product_name = "Nikon D70" />
  </constraint>
</topic>
```

In this example, the user query text is in the *query* field and the manually extracted AV constraints based on the domain model are in the *constraint* field. Two types of constraints are distinguished: hard and soft. The hard constraints must be satisfied while the soft constraints can be relaxed. Manual determination of hard vs. soft constraints is based on the linguistic features in the text. Automatic constraint extraction goes one step beyond AV extraction for the need to identify relations between attributes and values, for example, "nothing higher than" indicates a "<=" relationship. Such constraints can be extracted automatically from natural text using a pattern-based method. However, we have yet to produce a rich set of patterns addressing constraints. In addition, such query capability can be simulated with a form-based parametric search interface.

In order to make a fair comparison between systems, we use only phrases in the manually extracted constraints as queries to system S1. For the example topic, S1 extracted the NP terms "SLR", "1500" and "Nikon D70". During retrieval, a term is further decomposed into its subterms for similarity matching. For instance, the term "Nikon D70" is decomposed into subterms "Nikon" and "D70" and thus documents that mention the individual subterms can be retrieved.

For this topic, the system S2 produced annotations as those shown in the *constraint* field.

Table 1 gives a summary of the distribution statistics of terms and constraints for 30 topics selected from the Digital Photography Review website.

	Average	Min	Max
No. of terms	13.2	2	31
No. of constraints	3.2	1	7
No. of hard constraints	2.4	1	6
No. of soft constraints	0.8	0	3
No. of string constraints	1.4	0	5
No. of numerical constraints	1.8	0	4

Table 1: Summary of the distribution statistics of terms and constraints in the test topics

4.2 Relevance Judgments

Instead of using human subjects to give relevance judgments for each document and query combination, we use a human annotator to mark up all AV pairs in each document, using the GATE annotation tool (Cunningham *et al*, 2002). The attribute set contains the 40 most important attributes for digital cameras based on automatically computed term distributions in our data set. The inter-annotator agreement (without annotator training) as measured by Kappa is 0.72, which suggests satisfactory agreement.

Annotating AV pairs in all documents gives us the capability of making relevance judgments automatically, based on the number of matches between the AV pairs in a document and the constraints in a topic. This automatic approach is reasonable because unlike TREC queries which are short and ambiguous, the queries in our application represent very specific information needs and are therefore much longer. The lack of ambiguity makes our problem closer to boolean search with structured queries like SQL than traditional IR search. In this case, a human assessor should give the same relevance judgments as our automatic system if they follow the same instructions closely. An example instruction could be "a document is relevant if it describes a digital camera whose specifications satisfy at least one constraint in the query, otherwise it is not relevant" (similar to the narrative field of a TREC topic).

We specify two levels of relevance: strict and relaxed. *Strict* means that all hard constraints of a topic have to be satisfied for a document to be relevant to the topic, whereas *relaxed* means that at least half of the hard constraints have to be satisfied. Soft constraints play no role in a relevance judgment. The advantage of the automatic approach is that when the levels of relevance are modified for different application purposes, the relevance judgment can be recomputed easily, whereas in the manual approach, the human assessor has to examine all documents again.

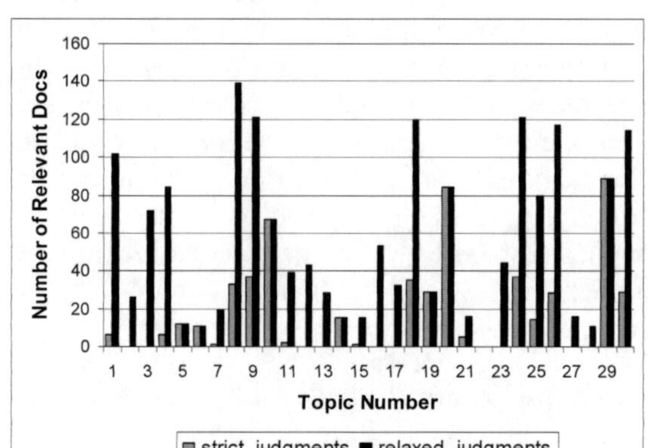

Figure 1: Distribution of relevant documents across topics for relaxed and strict judgments

Figure 1 shows the distributions of the relevant documents for the test topic set. With strict judgments, only 20 out of the 30 topics have relevant documents, and among them 6 topics have fewer than 10 relevant documents. The topics with many constraints are likely to result in low numbers of relevant documents. The average numbers of relevant documents for the set are 57.3 for relaxed judgments, and 18 for strict judgments.

5 Results and Discussion

Our goal is to explore whether using semantic information would improve document retrieval, taking into account the errors introduced by semantic processing. We therefore evaluate two aspects of our system: the accuracy of AV extraction and the precision of document retrieval.

5.1 Evaluate AV Extraction

We tested the AV extraction system on a portion of the annotated documents, which contains 253 AV pairs. Of these pairs, 151 have string values, and the rest have numerical values.

The result shows a prediction accuracy of 50.6%, false negatives (missing AV pairs) 35.2%, false positives 11%, and wrong predications 3%. Some attributes such as *brand* and *resolution* have higher extraction accuracy than other attributes such as *shooting mode* and *dimension*. An analysis of the missing pairs reveals three main sources of error: 1) an incomplete domain model, which misses such camera Condition phrases as "minor surface scratching"; 2) a noisy domain model, due to the automatic nature of its construction; 3) parsing errors caused by free-form human written texts. Considering that the predication accuracy is calculated over 40 attributes and that no human labor is involved in constructing the domain model, we consider our approach a satisfactory first step toward exploring the AV extraction problem.

5.2 Evaluate AV-based Document Retrieval

The three retrieval systems (S1, S2, and S3) each return top 200 documents for evaluation. Figure 2 summarizes the precision they achieved against both the relaxed and strict judgments, measured by the standard TREC metrics (*PN* – Precision at N, *MAP* – Mean Average Precision, *RP* – R-Precision)[1]. For both judgments, the combined system S3 achieved higher precision and recall than S1 and S2 by all metrics. In the case of recall, the absolute scores improve at least nine percent. Table 2 shows a pairwise comparison of the systems on three of the most meaningful TREC metrics, using paired T-Test; statistically significant results are highlighted. The table shows that the improvement of S3 over S1 and S2 is significant (or very nearly) by all metrics for the relaxed judgment. However, for the strict judgment, none of the improvements are significant. The reason might be that one third of the topics have no relevant documents in our data set. This reduces the actual number of topics for evaluation. In general, the performance of all three systems for the strict judgment is worse than that for the relaxed, likely due to the lower number of relevant documents for this category (averaged at 18 per topic), which makes it a harder IR task.

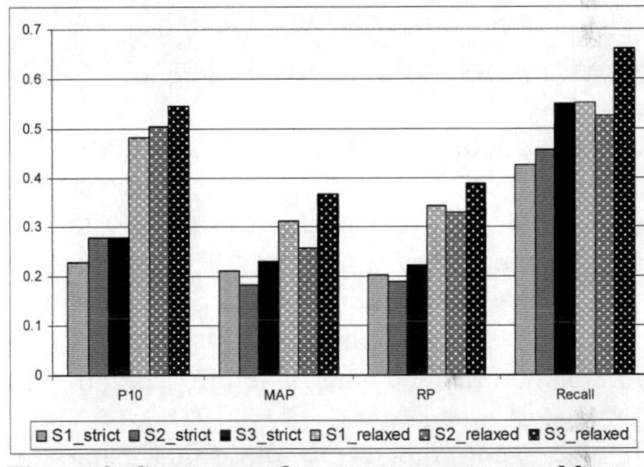

Figure 2: System performance as measured by TREC metrics, averaged over all topics with non-zero relevant documents

Paired T-Test (p)		*P10*	*AP*	*RP*
strict	(S1,S2)	.22	.37	.65
	(S2,S3)	1	**.004**	.10
	(S1,S3)	.17	.48	.45
relaxed	(S1,S2)	.62	.07	.56
	(S2,S3)	.056	**<.0001**	**.0007**
	(S1,S3)	**.04**	**.02**	**.03**

Table 2: Paired T-Test (with two-tailed distribution) between systems over all topics

The constraint-based system S2 produces higher initial precision than S1 as measured by P10. However, semantic constraints contribute less and less as more documents are retrieved. The performance of S2 is slightly worse than S1 as measured by AP and RP, which is likely due to errors from AV extraction. None of the metrics is statistically significant.

[1] Precision at N is the precision at N document cutoff point; Average Precision is the average of the precision value obtained after each relevant document is retrieved, and Mean Average Precision is the average of AP over all topics; R-Precision is the precision after R documents have been retrieved, where R is the number of relevant documents for the topic.

Topic-by-topic analysis gives us a more detailed view of the behavior of the three systems. Figure 3 shows the performance of the systems measured by P10, sorted by that of S3. In general, the performance of S1 and S2 deviates significantly for individual topics. However, the combined system, S3, seems to be able to boost the good results from both systems for most topics. We are currently exploring the factors that contribute to the performance boost.

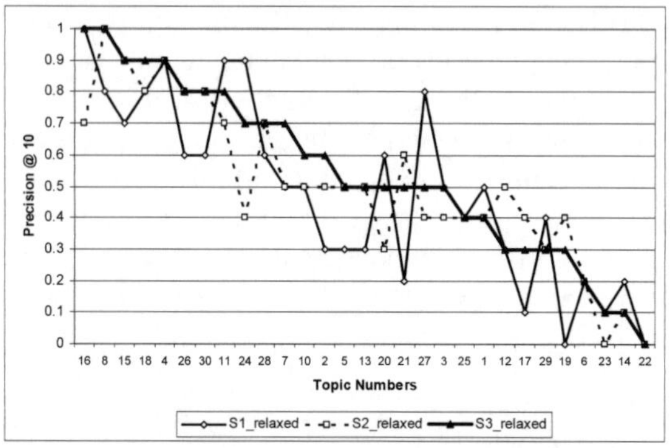

Figure 3: Precision@10 for relaxed judgment

A closer look at topics where S3 improves significantly over S1 and S2 at P10 reveals that the combined lists are biased toward the documents returned by S2, probably due to the higher scores assigned to documents by S2 than those by S1. This suggests the need for better score normalization methods that take into account the advantage of each system.

In conclusion, our results show that using semantic information can improve IR results for special domains where the information need can be specified as a set of semantic constraints. The constraint-based system itself is not robust enough to be a standalone IR system, and has to be combined with a term-based system to achieve satisfactory results. The IR results from the combined system seem to be able to tolerate significant errors in semantic annotation, considering that the accuracy of AV-extraction is about 50%. It remains to be seen whether similar improvement in retrieval can be achieved in general domains such as news articles.

6 Summary

This paper describes our exploratory study of applying semantic constraints derived from attribute-value pair annotations to traditional term-based document retrieval. It shows promising results in our test domain where users have specific information needs. In our ongoing work, we are expanding the test topic set for the strict judgment as well as the data set, improving AV extraction accuracy, analyzing how the combined system improves upon individual systems, and exploring alternative ways of combining semantic constraints and terms for better retrieval.

References

Hamish Cunningham, Diana Maynard, Kalina Bontcheva and Valentin Tablan. 2002. GATE: A Framework and Graphical Development Environment for Robust NLP Tools and Applications. *Proceedings of the 40th Anniversary Meeting of the Association for Computational Linguistics (ACL'02)*. Philadelphia.

Bruce Croft, James Callan and John Broglio. 1994. TREC-2 Routing and Ad-Hoc Retrieval Evaluation Using the INQUERY System. In *Proceedings of the 2nd Text Retrieval Conference*, NIST Special Putlication 500-215.

David A. Evans and Robert Lefferts. 1995. CLARIT-TREC experiments. *Information Processing and Management*, 31(3), 385-395.

E. Fix and J. Hodges. 1951. *Discriminatory Analysis, Nonparametric Discrimination: Consistency Properties*. Technical Report, USAF School of Aviation Medicine, Texas.

Joon Ho Lee. 1997. Analyses of Multiple Evidence Combination. Proceedings of the 20th Annual International ACM-SIGIR Conference on Research and Development in Information Retrieval. Philadelphia, pp. 267-276.

Dekang Lin. 1998. Dependency-based Evaluation of MINIPAR. *Workshop on the Evaluation of Parsing Systems*, Spain.

Yan Qu, David A. Hull, Gregory Grefenstette, David A. Evans, et al. 2005. Towards Effective Strategies for Monolingual and Bilingual Information Retrieval: Lessons Learned from NTCIR-4. *ACM Transactions on Asian Language Information Processing*, 4(2): 78-110.

Robert Wagner and Michael Fischer. 1974. The String-to-string Correction Problem. *Journal of the Association for Computing Machinery*, 21(1):168-173.

Tomek Strzalkowski, Louise Guthrie, Jussi Karigren, Jim Leistensnider, et al. 1996. Natural language information retrieval, TREC-5 report. In *Proceedings of the 5th Text Retrieval Conference (TREC-5)*, pp. 291-314, Gaithersburg, Maryland.

Ellen Voorhees. 1998. Using WordNet for text retrieval. In *Wordnet, an Electronic Lexical Database*, pp 285-303. The MIT Press.

Author Index

Association for Computational Linguistics
209 N. Eighth Street
Stroudsburg, Pennsylvania 18360

CURRAN ASSOCIATES INC
proceedings.com